CHAMPIONING ORGANIZATIONAL WELLNESS

COACHING TRIANGULATION OPTIMALLY POSITIONS LEADERS, ASPIRING LEADERS, AND ORGANIZATIONS TO EXCEL IN GLOBAL, MULTICULTURAL LANDSCAPES

ANTHONY L. SIMMONS, DSL, CAPTAIN, USN (RETIRED)

PAGE PUBLISHING
Conneaut Lake, PA

First originally published by Page Publishing 2023

eBook ISBN: 979-8-3481-1837-2

Paperback ISBN: 979-8-3481-1836-5

Printed in the United States of America

CONTENTS

PART 3 (WAYS): RELOCATING TO GAIN OPTIMAL POSITIONING: COACH AND COACHEE SYMMETRICAL ASCENSION THROUGH CULTURE AGNOSTICISM AND EMPOWERMENT THROUGH A COACHING ORGANIZATION

Part 4 (Ends): Conclusion

FOREWORD

After serving in the Navy for thirty-two years in a multitude of leadership positions, it was not until I served in USS *Lassen* as Captain Simmons's senior leadership advisor (command master chief) that I was enlightened on the true essence of developing talent inside an organization. First and foremost, I am honored to endorse Captain Simmons's work as these lessons and examples of a coaching organization he has presented herein have catapulted me and countless fellow shipmates and understudies to new heights and has been integral to the success of myriad Navy organizations. Giving this book a foreword affords me an opportunity to highlight my personal experience of enabling the success of leaders, aspiring leaders, and organizations through a platform of *championing organizational wellness* in USS *Lassen*.

While serving in *Lassen*, Captain Simmons infused me with a deeply profound desire to search within myself, to be the best man, leader, and father possible. His teachings crystallized and enabled me to not only work for four admirals but manage sailors on a higher level of leadership and mentoring. After serving with Captain Simmons, exhibiting leadership at my next commands, which employed ten thousand and forty-two thousand military and civilian personnel, respectively, seemed routine. Also, he held me accountable to standards much higher than what I had ever been accustomed to prior to serving with him. That lesson within itself was a crucial pivot, mind shift, and paradigm shift in my growth and development that will endure for a lifetime!

Furthermore, Captain Simmons was pivotal to my success by establishing an intricately moral atmosphere. One that kept over three hundred sailors focused with zeal, professionalism, and obedience. Being a product of such an amazing environment under Captain Simmons employed the vision and thought process for sailors and myself to always perform at the highest level imaginable. His leadership-coaching approach was paramount to cultivating my capacity to oversee the growth and development of every crew member in *Lassen* while I performed as their senior-enlisted advocate.

As a direct result of Captain Simmons's leadership, *Lassen*'s sailors were able to enjoy a plethora of successes. Particularly, he developed one sailor to win at the Pacific Fleet level Sailor-of-the-Year competition as she was selected among a group of ninety thousand eligible sailors for the prestigious award. This was immediately after his tenure; however, it was the infectious and enduring environment of success and achievements established by Captain Simmons that underscored this achievement. Owing to a culture laced with open dialogue, unearthing potential, and every crew member having a fair chance to excel and reaching for untapped potential within themselves, numerous sailors enjoyed their selection for many all-Navy sports programs, advancement, selection-to-officer programs, and earned college degrees.

Not only did Captain Simmons coach others to achieve at greater levels, but he also had an uncanny ability to make individuals look inside and discover their best selves. To substantiate his unparalleled culture of empowerment, Captain Simmons was an expert at equipping sailors to assume expanded responsibilities that led to *Lassen* achieving unprecedented successes across myriad operational and administrative tasks. His leadership coaching led to *Lassen*'s recognition as one of the most combat ready (battle efficient) ships in the United States Seventh Fleet. Essentially, the organization's many successes hinged on his leadership-coaching model of empowering others to excel at the highest level through responsibility, accountability, loyalty, and trust.

As I have captured how Captain Simmons impacted me, the crew, and the ship in this forwarding testimony, this narrative in and of itself personifies the essence of his book of *championing organizational wellness*. It illustrates how to link leaders and aspiring leaders to fostering a platform conducive to elevating and propelling everyone—despite his or her culture and social status—to new heights for organizational excellence.

Championing Organizational Wellness is not only a novel and assured model for leading across disparate cultures amid global landscapes but also the theory has been practiced and proven to position leaders, aspiring leaders, and organizations for optimal success through Captain Simmons's example in *Lassen*. Captain Simmons's natural ability to draw out the best in others through the model presented in this book continues to influence the growth and development of new leaders in countless organizations today.

—Master chief (retired) and author Leon Walker

PREFACE

This book is the culmination of my doctoral scholarship in strategic leadership at Regent University, coupled with my background of teaching leaders (executive since 1999) how to lead, which dates to my formative years as a student athlete. After embarking on my doctoral scholarship, I realized my work continued to reflect my innate leadership philosophy of leadership coaching, hence teaching leaders how to lead. My experience as an at-sea leader with expansive global experience, encompassing leadership engagements and visits to sixty-three countries, along with the vast research accomplished during my doctoral studies, makes me uniquely qualified to share leadership coaching concepts and methodologies to underscore leading amid disparate cultures in global expanses. Specifically, this work leverages my nautical acumen to present a *coaching triangulation* model on leadership coaching to mark the location of leaders, aspiring leaders, and points "true north" for disparate cultures in global-defense sectors to achieve organizational wellness. This model was derived from the triangulation methodology because it represents the most accurate way to fix one's position.

After serving in the Navy for twenty-eight years as a surface warfare officer and being afforded the honor of four at-sea commands, I found organizational wellness to be the apex for leadership at sea. The underlying methodologies for achieving this apex were based on building trusting relationships through a coaching environment that facilitated symmetrical learning between leaders and aspiring leaders. My goal was to foster a platform to facilitate organizational development and organizational sustainment as the aggregate of two realizes organizational wellness. As well, this coaching platform proved viable as over twenty-five of my understudies attained positions as at-sea commanders.

Leadership is at a point of inflection amid managing across multiple generations and cultures. It is more important now than ever for leaders to develop symbiotic and autotelic relationships with aspiring leaders. These relationships of mutual interest will bode well for developing trust and openness across these disparate groups. How do we manage this new direction?

Perhaps leadership is no longer the operative term for leading today's generations in global, multicultural landscapes, where employees and clients are less inclined to relegate themselves as mere followers. I suggest a coaching platform as the panacea for this new direction as it enables symmetrical growth for both the leader and aspiring leader. Coaching places the leader and aspiring leader on an elevated platform, so both may share a common perspective and an expanded vision for optimal organizational performance. I credit this elevated platform as the vehicle for the success of the aspiring leaders that I had the honor to coach.

PART 1

INTRODUCTION AND LITERATURE REVIEW

CHAPTER 1
Introduction

Championing Organizational Wellness evolves from a leadership coaching design to optimize the performance of leaders, aspiring leaders, and organizations holistically. New Age human interaction calls for relationships of coequals throughout organizations, whereas the operative term is *"coaching"* which is accentuated by shared goals between leaders, aspiring leaders, and organizations.[1] Although this book targets the global-defense sector, it also applies to myriad professions working amid diverse landscapes of global expanses. The book offers a firsthand account based on my personal visits and engagements with foreign dignitaries as a professional mariner. It explores matters beyond the leadership status quo by applying a *coaching* concept as the most viable solution to the most pressing challenges associated with leading diverse groups and cultivating aspiring leaders into new leaders. Just as I feel everyone should aspire to become a leader, this coaching construct is the catalyst to championing the path for aspiring leaders. In addition to encouraging continuous growth, *Championing Organizational Wellness* nurtures a culture of excellence through intentional and concerted professional development for organizational members indiscriminate of group affiliation.

Unlike leadership, mentoring, and counseling, coaching enhances organizational performance by bolstering human skills that are critical in multicultural, global landscapes. A human and organizational performance optimizer, coaching culminates into an intrinsic organizational leadership succession plan. Derived from positive psychology, coaching personifies an enduring relationship between the coach and coachee.[2] This lifelong relationship is predicated on empowering others to lead. In that spirit, this book refers to followers, coachees, clients, and employees as "aspiring leaders."

Leadership coaching was introduced in the 1960s by Paul Hersey and Kenneth Blanchard (https://www.edenproject.com). It involves a lifelong relationship of continuous growth among the coach, coachee, and organization through a cycle of generating new leaders to succeed their incumbents.[3] The evolution of leadership coaching became rapid at the turn of the twenty-first century as Katherine and Alex Szabo founded the Association for Coaching (AC), which represents the first dedicated body for professional coaching.[4] Since, the market value of the global leadership coaching industry was fifteen billion dollars, with $7.5 billion market value in the United States alone. The projected yearly growth rate is 6.7 percent (https://www.hellyescoachingonline.com/coaching-is-a-multi-billion-dollar-industry/). How does this growth link to organizational wellness?

In the '80s, managers were charged with managing the performance and satisfaction of their team members directly owing to human resources (HR) being transformed into a support model.[5] The efficacy of the managing performance was predicated on communication, interpersonal skills, and a coaching style. However, professional coaching was scarce and limited to those at the top of the organization while talented employees were assigned mentors for professional development whereas less-talented employees consulted with employee counselors.[6] This book not only serves to overcome this disjointed leadership development structure, but it also illustrates how to develop employees indiscriminate of position. How does leadership coaching take root inside organizations?

In organizations of diverse generational, ethical, or social cultures, coaching is the linchpin to connecting the respective cultural links. In this work, you will find a template that helps leaders coach aspiring leaders from the vantage point of the aspiring leader. The template is an educational tool to help leadership coaches identify their own location in relation to the location of the coachee. This scholarship affords a unique blueprint for building trust, symbiotic relationships between leaders and aspiring leaders throughout organizations, independent of cultural disposition. This blueprint is the *coaching triangulation model* which encapsulates an ends-means-ways operational design to capture and measure the progress of the coach, coachee, and organization holistically.

Problem statement

Because of today's volatile, uncertain, complex, and ambiguous (VUCA) environments, global connectedness, and the propensity for constant change in leadership, organizations must embrace methodologies to implement systemic leadership development practices to foster upward mobility amid disparate cultures. Under traditional leadership structures and practices, organizations lack the wherewithal to impartially champion the career of employees, owing to in-group favoritisms, behavioral ethics, and cultural disconnects/disparities. If not adequately addressed, these disparities could function as barriers to the application of the five components of emotional intelligence (EI) which are self-awareness, self-regulation, interpersonal skills, empathy, and motivation.[7] These components must be recognized and sharpened to upend these lingering barriers. EI components, coupled with self-assessments, allow leaders to identify with their own location while attaining the capacity to gauge the location of aspiring leaders independent of their ethical and cultural dispositions.

Unless they embody the capacity to identify with an aspiring leader's ethical and cultural dispositions, leaders are incapable of motivating and displaying empathy toward those from disparate cultures or ethnicity. Therefore, it is incumbent on leaders to identify with locations of aspiring leaders from their respective vantage points. Cultural disparities must be ameliorated through a leadership coaching intervention to judge the distance between leaders and aspiring leaders. In addition to the components of EI and assessments, navigating blind spots and a coaching conversation homogenize the locations of the leaders and aspiring leaders. Once a homogeneous location is realized, culture agnosticism and a coaching culture illuminate the path(ways) for optimal coach, coachee, and organizational performance. Accordingly, *coaching triangulation* is leveraged to oversee the interactions between the coach and coachee and to realize organizational wellness. Again, this organizational end state is the aggregate of organizational development and sustainment.

Organizational wellness must be intentional and sought out because too often organizations enlist initiatives to encourage leadership development and career championing across all groups but eventually fail at sustaining the process when leadership changes. I would submit the change in leadership introduces new blind spots, blind motivation, and ethical dilemmas that manifest differences in perspective, eventually driving the organization in different directions. *Coaching triangulation* precludes this behavior by equipping new leaders, despite cultural beliefs and values, with an organizational wellness construct to readily suppress these behaviors/tendencies to sustain the direction of the organization. Moreover, the model enables leaders to relate to aspiring leaders by interacting with them based on a known location comprised of a nexus to enable social, ethical, and cultural integration. The *coaching triangulation* methodology encompasses encapsulating the relationship between the leadership coach, aspiring leader, and organization and ultimately exemplifies a framework which facilitates their performance apex—organizational wellness!

Approach/methodology: Coaching triangulation design model

Where is the coach? Where is the coachee? How does their symmetrical movement optimize the organization's position? How do the coach and coachee move symmetrically to position the leader, the aspiring leader, and the organization for success? *Coaching triangulation* entails fixing locations of coach and coachee to cultivate a strategic path for HR development and organizational success. Organizational success is predicated on the projected movement of the coach and coachee as the three embrace a set of shared goals.[8] *Coaching triangulation* is fitting to capture these interactions necessitated to realize these shared goals.

This work leverages the coaching triangle provided in Figure 1 to capture the interrelationship between the coach and coachee and how they shape organizational wellness amid disparate groups through the application of EI, assessments, suppressing blind spots, and coaching conversation through being culturally agnostic and building coaching organizations.

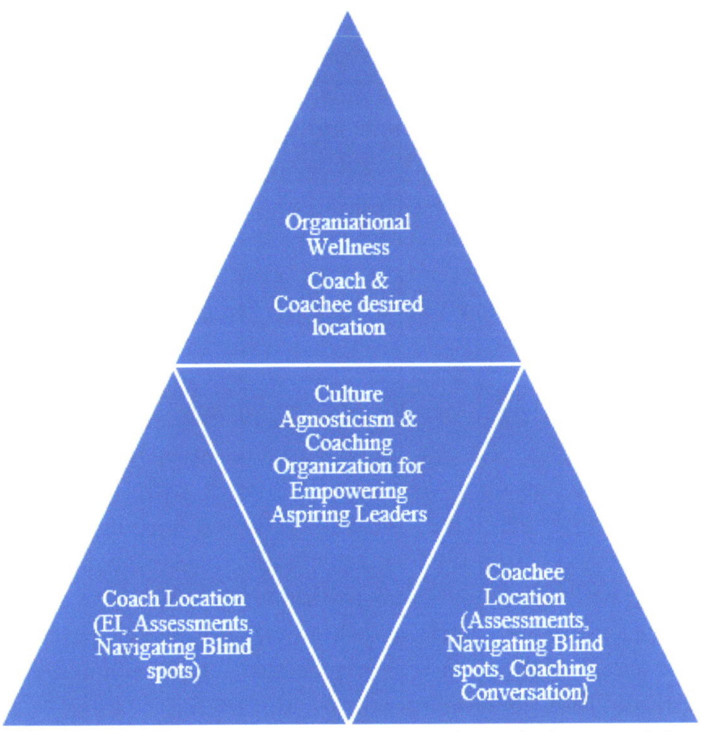

Figure 1. Conceptual coaching triangulation model

Global landscapes demand organizations to adopt leadership coaching methodologies conducive to developing aspiring leaders of disparate social, ethical, and cultural backgrounds. This research expands on leadership theories through a coaching construct to depict the locations of leaders, aspiring leaders, and organization to optimize the performance for all. Accordingly, I have designed a *coaching triangulation* methodology to capture the ingredients/components for organizational coaching using an ends-means-ways operational design model. This methodology will afford leaders a vehicle to master the dynamics of leading across diverse cultures and bolster their efficacy for establishing level-playing fields. By superimposing the operational design model on a coaching triangle, I have established a common landscape for leaders and aspiring leaders while leveraging my hands-on experience to illustrate how leadership efficacy is realized through coaching intervention and culture agnosticism. The genesis of this model links back to my days fixing ships' positions in global maritime environments.

When hiking or backpacking without a geospatial positioning system (GPS) device, there are a few ways to pinpoint one's exact location on a map. The most reliable and accurate method to determine location without GPS is using triangulation, a simple technique that can usually narrow whereabouts down to a radius of as little as ten meters. This technique consists of observing the direction or bearing of (two or) three landmarks characterizing the corners of a triangle with the pinpointed location somewhere within that triangle.[9] The Navy uses triangulation to fix ships' positions and determine optimal courses for safe maneuvering.

Coaching triangulation was conceived from this concept as fixing a coachee's location to design an optimal course for professional development. Leadership coaching, identifying with one's position regardless of culture difference, is essential to determining the path for success. The key to fixing positions accurately is using points that are distinguished, which is why it's key to first identify with the leader and aspiring leader's locations and the desired position of the organization. Once these initial positions are clearly defined, the coach and coachee can determine their relative positions inside the triangle. *Coaching triangulation* personifies the leader's and aspiring leaders' location as they move symmetrically as a composite unit to achieve optimal performance for all parties.

Ends-means-ways operational design

Richard Yarger posits strategy is centered on the ways leaders apply means at their disposal to manage circumstances to achieve ends.[10] *Coaching triangulation* involves the application of EI, assessments, navigating blind spots, and coaching conversation as the means for the coach and coachee to grow symmetrically and optimally impact the organizational performance. These ways comprise how the coach and coachee interact amid diverse cultures and a coaching intervention to achieve the ends—optimize their growth and organizational performance.

EI, assessments, and navigating blind spots are foundational competencies (means) for leadership coaching while the coaching conversation yields a call-to-action. The aggregate of the means sets the stage for applying filters (ways) to navigate inside the coaching triangle to realize organizational wellness as illustrated in Figure 2. While EI and assessments set the course for navigating blind spots, the renewed vision that results from removing blind spots is the catalyst to building a trusting relationship that accentuates the coaching conversation. Once the means have taken root, the ways can then be manifested as culture agnosticism and a coaching culture are dependent on unbiased views or suspended ethical approaches to leadership development. Coaching organizational wellness represents the apex of *coaching triangulation* but moreover positions the coachee to succeed the coach through cycling back through the triangle from the coach's location as depicted in Figure 2. To summarize this concept, the components inside the coaching triangle illustrate how coaching organizational wellness coalesces into a comprehensive picture for developing and sustaining global leaders amid disparate cultures.

Figure 2. Coaching triangulation model

It is worth noting the third point (apex) of the triangle is unconventional as it is derived for reverse navigation or assuming the ideal position for optimal growth for the coach, coachee, and organization. This performance apex is predicated on the efficacy of the ways inside the triangle. If cultural agnosticism is achieved and a coaching culture is established, the position is readily attainable.

Effectively, the apex manifests from both the coach and coachee moving in symmetry amid the ways to achieve organizational wellness.

Coaching triangulation characterizes a closed-loop system because the coachee embodies the same skills as the coach once she/he reaches the apex of the triangle. The coachee becomes the coach's successor and is prepared to repeat the cycle by repositioning at the coach's original starting position. *Organizational wellness* is the confluence of organizational development and organizational sustainment, hence the culmination of the design which represents the desired end state.

Coaching advantage: Benefits of a coaching organization

Making others better has always been easy for me; it's my modus operandi!

Reading this book will imbue defense-industry leaders with tools to realize efficacy in leadership roles across disparate cultures, whereas the efficacy of their leadership depends on social rhetorical locations. It will develop experts in global environment by yielding culturally agnostic leadership coaches. As well, this resource is pivotal to an organization's capacity to align leaders and aspiring leaders so they may move in lockstep to realize organizational wellness. It removes blind spots so leaders and aspiring leaders can share a common lens to symmetrically determine the best path for mutual success.

Historically, organizational wellness ebbed and flowed based on the disposition of executive leadership. This work triumphs this trend by providing a coaching platform that facilitates organizational design where collective leadership development supplants individualism to sustain first-rate performance. This coaching intervention normalizes the work environment and career opportunities for all by linking the location of the leader with the aspiring leader. So regardless of the executive leader's background, the fundamental design of the model allows symmetrical growth indiscriminately. *Coaching triangulation* equips leaders with requisite apparatus to overcome individualistic shortcomings, such as blind spots, by assessing their tendencies against organizational needs. It tests what ought to be done against what leaders are comfortable doing.[11]

How often have diversity initiatives been implemented to level career opportunities before failing when leadership changes? Why did previous initiatives fail? Where do we go from here? Too often organizations begin initiatives to underscore leadership development and career championing across all groups but eventually fail at sustaining the desired outcome. I would surmise the failure is likely associated with changes in executive leadership, whereas the leader's vision and culture drive the organization in a different direction. *Coaching triangulation* injects the leader, despite ethical background, cultural beliefs, and behavioral ethics, into the organizational wellness construct to sustain the direction of the organization holistically. Specifically, it offers a template where leaders of any culture/ethnicity can be inserted into the model and achieve the same organizational performance outcome. As well, the model allows the leader to relate to the aspiring leader by interacting through known locations or baseline interactions on common locations.

Accordingly, this book leverages a *coaching triangulation* model to capture *the relationship between the coach, coachee, and the organizational vision. This vision coincides with organization wellness.* It serves to reshape the organizational landscape across employees independent of backgrounds to optimize performance. To avoid disruptions in talent management, it fosters career championing for those who hail from different backgrounds by eradicating blind spots and cultural differences through applying the means resident in the coaching triangle.

Why coaching over leading, counseling, and mentoring? What separates coaching from these approaches? Coaching leverages the International Coaching Federal (ICF) core competences to develop learning machines that are strategic HR imperatives for organizational success.[12] Coaching unearths the emotional space to help coachees feel better from within—it is intimate and introspective. The concept is distinguished by an enduring relationship between coequals where they can mutually influence the progress of one another. Table 1 below provides a comparison of attributes (https://christiancoaches.com/wp-content/uploads/2017/10/Competencies-Edited-Final-2017.pdf).[13]

Coaching	Counseling	Mentoring	Leading
Positive Psychology	Negative Psychology	Neutral Psychology	Positive Psychology
Influencing	Uplifting	Imparting	Directing

Broad	Focused	Less Broad	Focused
Progression	Security	Facilitating	Imparting
Coequals	Advisor	Leader-Follower	Leader-Follower
Perpetual	Episodic	Episodic	Circumstantial

Table 1. Comparable table for coaching,
counseling, mentoring, and leading

Not only is coaching catalyst to executive leaders' growth, but it also ensures their professional development is deliberate and intentional. It removes the cultural scar tissues or ambiguity and ambivalence from career championing. Instead, career championing is a part of the organizational design across all cultures/groups. This is done by coaching leaders on how to lead as the process yields perpetual growth for all—the leader, client, and organization.

This process is a strategic HR imperative as it underpins career championing for in-group and out-group entities; it enables group agnosticism. This work affords leadership coaches a guidebook for championing the careers of aspiring leaders despite their origin or ethnicity. Although the book is paramount for global-defense leaders, normalizing leadership coaching processes by championing the careers of future leaders independent of cultures and catapulting organizational wellness, the blueprint is also applicable to sports, education, and corporate sectors. The model can be altered by substituting the appropriate filter to address a multitude of professions. Moreover, the book offers a continuous, closed-loop process for leadership development and succession for sustained organizational wellness.

Book overview: Achieving organizational wellness through coaching triangulation

The book consists of four: Part 1: The Introduction and Literature Review; Part 2 (Means): Coach and Coachee Locations: Location of Coach and Coachee through Five Components of Emotional Intelligence and Assessments, Navigating Blind Spots, and Coaching Conversation ; Part 3 (Ways): Relocating to Gain Optimal Positioning: Coach and Coachee Symmetrical Ascension through Culture

Agnosticism and Empowerment through a Coaching Organization; and Part 4 (Ends): Conclusion. The following paragraph illustrates the layout of this book.

In this chapter, I have discussed leadership coaching, the problem it solves, and how the *coaching triangulation* methodology superimposed on the ends-means-ways operational design is appropriate for achieving organizational wellness amid disparate cultures. The model is catalyst to the leader and aspiring leader ascending symmetrically to reach organizational wellness in unison. Chapter 2 offers a literature review as the underpinning and overarching perspective on leadership coaching across the global-defense sector. Starting with chapter 3, the book distills down on how this triangulation model works in concert to arrive at this apex for sustained organization performance across a multicultural defense industry. Specifically, in chapter 3, the coaches' location is marked through the five components of emotional intelligence and self-assessments. Then chapter 4 expands on this location by helping the coach examine and challenge embedded blind spots which may have originated from EI and values deficiencies, misaligned values, generational disparities, cultural biases/disconnects, or ethnical behaviors. Once the distance between coach and coachee are determined, chapter 5 comprises/introduces the coaching conversation which allows the coach and coachee to move in the right direction symmetrically through intuitive listening, asking powerful questions, designing actions, and supporting the process.

In chapter 6, cultural agnosticism is realized through cultural ingratiation, culture competence, and culture agility. In chapter 7, I will illustrate how to establish a culture of coaching through empowering others through servantship, five practices of exemplary leadership and democratized leadership. The book concludes in chapter 8 by illustrating what organizational wellness (OW) entails by offering organizational development (OD) and organizational sustainment (OS) resources which include strategic communications, Strategic Human Resource Development, coach-protégé programs, and intermediate performance reviews as the culmination of *coaching triangulation*. The blueprint concludes with a high-performance continuum which fancy as an autonomous leadership succession plan.

CHAPTER 2
Literature Review

Abstract

This chapter gives an overview of the myriad aspects of executive coaching in the global-defense industry by defining the term, reviewing the history and theoretical base of coaching, and highlighting how it has evolved into a catalyst for global-defense leaders. Establishing common grounds among diverse cultures through coaching interventions is an imperative for bridging people of diverse cultures along the information highway; it integrates people and technology to optimize and sustain global organizations' performance despite cultural differences. In addition to aligning culture norms and capitalizing on technological advances, coaching helps leaders grow new leaders and draw out skills to build successions without losing sight of organizational goals and objectives.

Introduction

This review illustrates how coaching in the global-defense sector builds unified coalitions through successful organizations to best support global security through wielding forces into one vision. At the turn of the twenty-first century, the market value of the leadership coaching industry was fifteen billion dollars, with a $7.5 billion worth market value in the United States alone. The projected yearly growth rate is 6.7 percent (https://www.hellyescoachingonline.com/coaching-is-a-multi-billion-dollar-industry/). It truly evolved at the beginning of the century to pace the many changes and complexity of leading across global environments in multiple industries; the defense sector is highlighted herein. Coaching involves a lifelong relationship of continuous growth for the coach, the coachee, and the organization through the development of new leaders possessing requisite skills to succeed incumbent leaders.[14] Coaching is shaped by cultures,[15] so this process bodes well for organizations in global expanses in the defense sector because it enables alignment among disparate cultures and the insight and foresight to recognize changes in global markets in time to capitalize on opportunities and warn off threats.

Some definitions of executive leadership coaching

Founded in 1995 to conduct a worldwide campaign for coaching standards, the International Coaching Federation (ICF) defines coaching as partnering with clients in a thought-provoking and creative form which inspires them to maximize their personal and professional attributes (https://coachingfederation.org/history). Leadership coaching is a teaching method for fostering mature relationships, healthier thinking, and optimal decision-making amid disparate groups for those in leadership roles (http://www.wisegeek.net/what-is-leadership-coaching.htm).

The McLean Institute of coaching defines coaching as an invaluable tool for developing people across a wide range of needs and of tremendous benefit to organizations at large (https://instituteofcoaching.org).

Coaching is a collaborative process that alters perceptions and behavior patterns so people can effectively adapt to and accept change as a challenge rather than an obstacle.[16]

Coaching is a leadership continuum consisting of developing, reshaping, and refining leaders continuously so they may reach their optimal level of performance across complex and changing external actors. Coaching is a skill applied to assist individuals to see inside themselves to determine how their values align to their vision and for assisting disparate organizations to look beyond individual beliefs to coalesce mutual strengths. Coaching is the integral of leadership because it allows leaders to grow to realize hidden talents that would otherwise fail to materialize; leadership is the derivative of coaching because coaching generates more leaders.

The history and theoretical base of executive coaching

The coaching leadership style was introduced in the 1960s by Paul

Hersey and Kenneth Blanchard as one of four leadership styles found in the Eden Project (www.edenproject.com). However, it's hard to pinpoint exactly when executive coaching first began outside literature that indicates the late 1980s.[17] But we do know the theory of coaching is a spin-off of positive psychology and serves to optimize human and organizational performance.[18] Coaching emerged on the premise of a client-based engagement underpinned by the coach embodying keen self-awareness, self-regulation, interpersonal skills, motivation, and empathy.[19] These components are not only enablers for the ICF process, they are also multipliers for moving clients from where they are to where they desire to reside. Initially, the coaching form of leadership was not in favor because of high pressure for organizations to achieve goals...developing people was considered too time-consuming (www.edenproject.com).

Forms of executive coaching

Coaching encapsulates three forms of leadership: situational, servant, and transformational. Despite have commonalities with these three forms of leadership, coaching is distinguished by its client-based approach consisting of intuitive listening, asking open-ended questions to enable the client's introspective, instituting a call to action to affirm finding, and engaging in ongoing efforts to support the realization of these actions.[20] Just as situational leadership is based on the level of engagement required, coaching engagements are predicated on the disposition of the coachee.[21] In accord with servant leadership, coaching is about elevating an individual to a higher state of being. And, finally, coaching transforms by allowing an individual to realize change from his/her own personal discovery through coaching conversations. Below are excerpts of these three leadership types as they relate to coaching.[22]

Situational leadership approach

This approach is incumbent on the coach to adapt his level of engagement to the demands of the coachee based on situations and conditions.[23] The more urgent the situation, the more involved the leader. Coaching is situational because it shares common threads with situational leadership models depicted below in Figure 3. The coaching process is resident in this model as the bridge between directing (leading, counseling, mentoring) to supporting and delegating. Effective coaching enables independent performers.

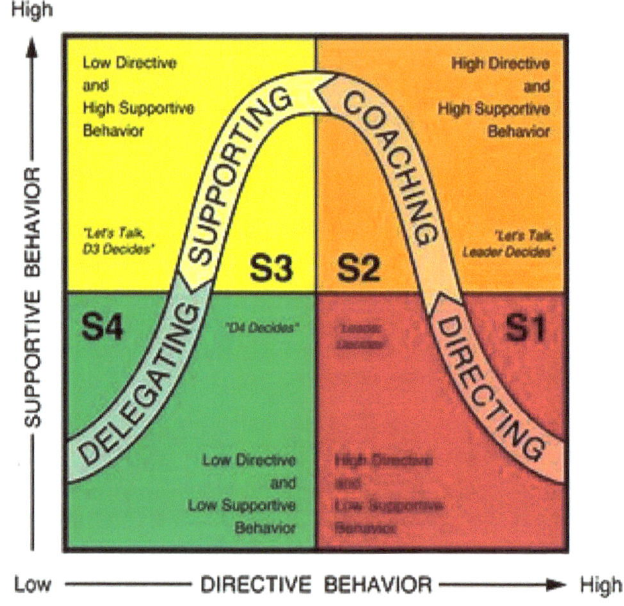

Figure 3. Leadership continuum of learning

Servant leadership approach

This approach, akin to a coaching relationship, places the interest of the follower at the forefront of the engagement. As resident in a coaching conversation, the leader must be attentive to the concerns of the follower, empathize, and nurture as necessary to enable his/her personal and professional growth.[24]

Transformational leadership approach

This approach mirrors coaching whereas this leadership process consists of individuals engaging other individuals to create a connection which elevate the level of motivation and morality in both the leader and followers akin to the coach and coachee.[25] Transformational coaching is the art of assisting people to enhance their effectiveness in a way they feel helped.[26]

The development and evolution of coaching

Coaching evolved from a "meme" or the transferring of ideas from one person to another.[27] Coaching is a leadership development option which had become more prevalent in the complex and changing landscape where EI has succumbed to AI. This is not a digital world, so human intervention (skill) is necessary if people are to adapt to environmental demands. Coaching develops leaders through listening, asking questions, calling to action, and supporting the transformation through servant leadership.[28] The four domains of leadership strength consist of executing, influencing, relationship building, and strategic thinking.[29] Influencing and relationship building are quintessential to drawing out attributes and expanding thinking while relationship building is catalyst to achieving wholeness and fostering trust. The evolution of coaching is best represented in Table 2 below by comparing its attributes to those of mentoring, counseling, mentoring, and leading.[30] As for leadership, it better serves to leverage the parallels as leadership is a derivative of coaching, which is paradoxical since leadership styles preceded coaching. Over time, statistics has proved executive coaching is a direct contributor to higher self-efficacy in executives.[31]

Coaching	Counseling	Mentoring	Leading
Positive Psychology	Negative Psychology	Neutral Psychology	Positive Psychology
Influencing	Uplifting	Imparting	Directing
Broad	Focused	Less Broad	Focused
Progression	Security	Facilitating	Imparting
Coequals	Advisor	Leader-Follower	Leader-Follower
Perpetual	Episodic	Episodic	Circumstantial

Table 2. Comparable table for coaching, counseling, mentoring, and leading

The coaching process

The International Coaching Federation (ICF) core competencies capture the coaching process in the following steps:

- *Setting the foundation*
  - Meeting ethical guidelines and professional standards—understanding and applying coaching ethics while communicating differences between coaching, consulting, psychotherapy, other support professions; referring clients for other professional help as warranted
  - Establishing the coaching agreement—understanding requirement for the coaching interaction and coming to agreement with the client about the process and relationship through discussing guidelines and responsibilities; ascertaining the appropriateness of the coaching match

- *Cocreating the relationship*
  - Establishing trust and intimacy with the client—creating a safe, supportive environment which produces trust and mutual respect through showing genuine concern for client's welfare, demonstrating integrity, honesty, and sincerity while establishing clear agreement and keeping promises; supports client as warranted and be sensitive toward certain areas
  - Coaching presence—being fully conscious, spontaneous with client through exuding openness, flexibility, and confident through intuitive listening, displaying wherewithal, and creating energy

- *Communicating effectively*
  - Active listening—focusing the client conversation to feel the underlying artifacts in the context of the client's desires to support his self-expression by attending to client's agenda, goals, values, and beliefs; being keen on nonverbal communications, reiterating and reflecting on clients' comments while encouraging and integrating thoughts

without passing judgment
- o Powerful questioning—asking relevant questions to reveal the requisite information to maximize the benefits of the relationship and client by asking open-ended questions from the client's perspective to evoke discovery, insight, and commitment to action to move clients toward their desires
- o Direct communication—communicating effectively to engender positive impact while sharing feedback to help clients see from different perspectives; clearly state objectives, meeting agenda, and purpose of techniques used to illustrate points and paint verbal pictures

- *Facilitating learning and results*
  - o Creating awareness—integrating, evaluating, and interpreting information bolster the client's awareness and achieve agreed-upon results; looking beyond concerns through thoughtful inquiry to inspire commitment, clarify perspectives, enable self-discovery, identify strengths against growth, and learn potential while helping client discern between trivial and significant and situational and recurring behaviors
  - o Designing actions—creating opportunities for continuous learning during work/life situations and taking new actions to yield agreed-upon results; define actions through brainstorming to deepen learning, systematically explore concerns, and explore alternative ideas through active-experimentation and self-discovery; celebrate success and future growth opportunities while advocating points of views that align with client goals and providing immediate support, thus observing a comfortable pace of learning
  - o Planning and goal setting—developing and maintaining effective coaching plan through collective relevant information and developing and actionable yet flexible coaching plan for learning and development
  - o Managing progress and accountability—be mindful of agreed-upon actions and leave responsibility with the client to execute; perform follow-up to track progress and fill any

gaps the client may experience with expectations and actions executed

The initial conversations for individual executive leaders who desires leadership coaching begins with a telephone consultation to determine the structure for the coaching. Regardless, the conversation during this conversation is kept confidential.

Coaching in the global-defense sector

Coaching is used in the defense industry to develop diverse leaders through a continuous learning process to adapt to high level of change and to align cultures in partnership engagement in support of global security.[32] The demand for constant change requires transformational leadership, which is best underscored by coaching.[33] A one-size-fits-all approach to leadership is ineffective in diverse environments, so the coaching approach—like leadership—must be in alignment with group values and the organizational construct.[34] Furthermore, coaching cultures operate as superior cultures with superior context and lead to exemplary organizational outcomes.[35] Coaching is a global, lifelong journey of reciprocating and nurturing relationships akin to the Apostle Paul's journey with his followers to ensure their growth and share how he learned from them as well.

How society, cultures, and values shape global coaching

Coaching should be approached from the perspective of respective cultures. It is best conducted among cultures who have more in common. The coaching relationship is more productive when the coach and the coachee has more in common.[36] In cases where cultures are vastly different, coaching must be done with the differences depicted in Table 3 below. A good approach is to consider whether an interaction is taking place in certain regions of the world where cultures are least inclined to communicate or share information. For example, military leaders must possess the wherewithal to identify with and adapt as necessary to culture types and dimensions to perform coaching across varying conditions.[37] The blended model provided in Table 3 is illustration of coaching approaches based on cultural constraints.[38]

Regardless, assessments are key to baselining individual coaching engagements.[39] Talent management in organizations across borders requires assessments of the respective leaders' global leadership competencies.[40]

	(Individualism-Collectivism	Egalitarian-Hierarchical	Traditional-Nontraditional	Expressive-Reserved	Coaching Approaches
Western	Individualism	Egalitarian	Nontraditional	Expressive	Collaborative
Middle Eastern	Individualism	Hierarchical	Traditional	Reserved	Instructional
Asia	Individualism	Hierarchical	Traditional	Reserved	Facilitative
Latin	Collectivism	Egalitarian	Traditional	Expressive	Instructional
Africa	Collectivism	Hierarchical	Nontraditional	Expressive	Instructional

Table 3: Cultural relationships comparisons

Coaches must establish common ground to gain an appreciation for diverse cultures and work toward common purposes. Bridging cultures is a matter of a recognizing cultural differences and coaching in ways that explicitly consider the differences to unify ideas and to coalesce values, beliefs, ideas, and behaviors.[41]

Ramifications for individuals

Coaching in the defense sector is critical because leaders can ill afford too much risk and must balance effectiveness with efficiencies. Coaching facilitates interaction to normalize disparate groups. Coaching is taking someone from where they are to where they desire to go through personal transformation that takes place through relational behavior, intuitive listening, influence, responsibility, accountability, and empowerment.[42] The result of this personal transformation yields unrivaled wisdom which, in turn, bolsters the components of EI.[43] This wisdom translates in wise ways of leadership which is about many leaders working together to achieve a common purpose—the overarching objective of global-security entities.[44] Coaching allows leaders to grow beyond being leaders and focus on developing new leaders without completely losing sight of the objectives.

Ramifications for organizations

Coaching in organization relies heavily on the pedigree of leadership, whereas the propensity for an organization to embrace coaching is dependent on the background of executive leadership.[45] Performing executive coaching is impetus for leaders to promote individual development and organizational learning to champion the organization's larger goals.[46] Individual coaching and organizational performance is related through team reflection or the sum of the whole.[47] The bottom line is organizations with coaching cultures possess the capability to meet external demands by developing internal agility. A coaching culture turns internal weaknesses into strengths and transforms external threats into opportunities.

Coaching programs for leaders in the global-defense sector

Executive leaders are using coaching because the rigors of leadership have prompted defense leaders to adopt a learning continuum to best manage their energy and fortify their character.[48] Senate Hearing 111-594 entitled "Developing Federal Employees and Supervisors: Mentoring, Internships, and Training in Federal Government" addresses providing federal employees with the tools they need to be successful.[49] Also it asserts mentoring as being integral to retaining a diverse workforce while parallel efforts are afoot to synchronize professional training and education of senior executives and flag officers to increase joint capability, which would be filtered down to the lowest level of the work force.[50]

Defense Acquisition University (DAU)

In 2009, the DAU launched an initiative to train experienced acquisition practitioners as executive coaches to create a long-term culture change of developing, mentoring, and coaching new leaders; hence, creating a learning enterprise (https://www.dau.edu/locations/dsmc/p/Executive-Coaching).

Below is a depiction of the executive coaching framework used in the defense sector for coaching executive leaders. This framework serves as a viable cross-reference for ICF core competencies, coaching conversation, situational leadership components, and the transformational leadership model.[51]

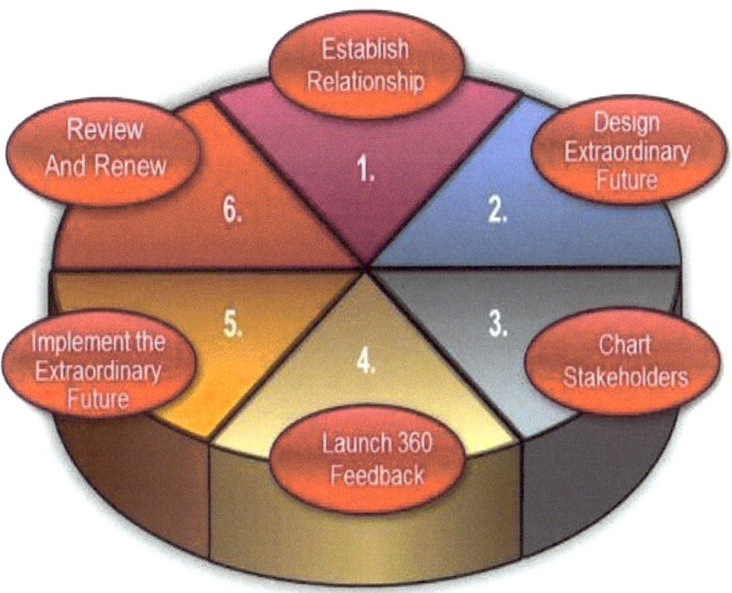

Benefits of coaching leaders in the global-defense sector

Coaching is a catalyst to seamless leadership succession in complex and changing environments. Coaching allows disparate cultures to grow into one common culture of mutual values and beliefs. This is done through elevating thinking to cultural adaptation and sensitivity, which are key components to global leadership.[52] The goal of leadership in the defense sector is to balance between achieving goals—in sometimes life-and-death situations—and developing new agile leaders capable of pacing change in complex and diverse landscapes. Coaching is key in the defense sector because it allows organizations to capitalize on or achieve return on investment (ROI) on the training provided to employees. A coaching culture improves retention and supports talent management, which is key to performance continuity. This is realized through persistently and systemically developing new leaders. The irony of leadership is 90 percent of leaders merely attract followers rather than develop leaders.[53]

Coaching produces agile global-defense leaders

Coaching is catalyst to overcoming cultural barriers for which CEOs feel have become more and more challenging. Coaching creates agile global leaders equipped to excel in multicultural environments. Leaders must be able to adapt to cultural norms, minimize cultures, and integrate into cultures depending on the situation.[54] Coaching-based leadership facilitates positive intervention to imbue leaders with the requisite skills to know which response is appropriate for optimal organizational performance among certain cultures.[55] The level of agility within organizations must match the level of agility necessary to answer ongoing global changes which requires more agile leaders.[56]

Coaching engenders trust

As we move rapidly in a more transparent, interdependent global reality, trust is the glue to make us one.[57] Furthermore, low trust slows decisions, blocks communication, and stifles relationships that are organizational imperatives in the global-defense industry.[58] This trust is manifested and sustained through coaching executive leaders on culture norms of allied countries, so expectations are aligned to common purposes based on understanding values and social behaviors. Trust resonates in action as there should be no light between one's words and deeds.[59]

Reasons global-defense sector leaders seek coaching

Global leaders are seeking coaching because the complexities and vagaries of different cultures demand expanded leadership skills that can be realized through coaching.[60] To perform successfully in global expanses depends on understanding and embracing the difference in cultures. Coaching is vital in global defense because of its nature of facilitating engagements of people from disparate cultures to draw out and better understand their motivation (www.edenproject.com). For example, the Asia-Pacific rapidly changing backdrop mandates leadership development in the defense sector, thus requiring ongoing education that relies on bilateral engagements with allied groups.[61]

Coaching is instrumental in bolstering global-defense leaders' professional development which underscores their professional ethos. It helps cultures grow together and helps each culture succeed at resolving national security issues. Extensive review on culture literature in relation to behaviors and practices concluded national and social culture is measured through a set of values reflecting what is important or desirable in the respective culture. It's critical for each culture to fully grasp this reality. For example, an alliance between American culture, which values individual economical wealth, and African culture, which values collective gain, to normalize perspectives.

The global leadership and organizational behavior effectiveness (GLOBE) study found culture to influence the type of leadership qualities that identify outstanding leadership. Particularly in cross-cultural perspectives, certain aspects (i.e., participative) of leadership are culturally contingent.[62] GLOBE is a standing program designed to conceptualize, operationalize, test, and validate cross-level integrated theory of relationship between culture and societal, organizational, and leadership effectiveness.[63] All for which are paramount to global leadership in the defense sector.

Coaching creates a scalable landscape to seamlessly embrace change

Coaching helps develop critical skills and leadership agility required to pace the high levels of change and complexity that constantly bombard organizations.[64] The scalability resonates in attaining leadership agility through developing interchangeable parts to meet unpredictable future threats.[65] Coaching helps to respond to competition by revamping, reshaping, and refining interpersonal skills to function in high technological environments and compete globally. Coaching yields measured change; ROI from coaching intervention is reflected by positive changes in employee orientation (working with people), task orientation, and improved personal behavior. Without coaching, organizations would be too rigid to pace change.[66]

Conclusion

The executive leadership coaching in the global-defense sector will afford continuous learning for diverse leaders to bridge both AI and EI and culture differences to enable sustained worldwide security through sharing uniform visions. Unlike leadership, which is goal-oriented, coaching, as Daniel Goleman shared with *New York Times*, is good for organizations willing to put up with short-term failure to further long-term learning (https://www.edenproject.com).

Coaching allows defense leaders to function in familiar territories regardless of how far from home they are. Nehemiah 8 and 9 reads: "Lord, please remember the promises made to Moses. You told him that if we were unfaithful, you would spread us among foreign nations. But you also said that no matter how far away we were, we could turn to you and start obeying your laws. Then you would bring us back to the place where you have chosen to be worshipped" (CEV). Coaching entails having faithful and trusting engagements with allies so that all lands appear monolithic.

PART 2
(MEANS)

COACH AND COACHEE LOCATIONS: LOCATION OF COACH AND COACHEE THROUGH FIVE COMPONENTS OF EMOTIONAL INTELLIGENCE AND ASSESSMENTS, AVIGATING BLIND SPOTS, AND COACHING CONVERSATION

Coaches must be coached, even if they are coached by the coachees.

—Anthony Simmons

CHAPTER 3

Emotional Intelligence and Assessments Realize Locations for Coach and Coachee

Coach, do you know where you are? Better yet, is it possible for you to locate and relate to others if you don't know your location? Not only do I consider these questions appropriate to shape the intent of this chapter, but also they suggest a follow-on question: how emotionally intelligent are you? Embodying a high degree of EI is one thing that all great leaders have in common.[67] Because of artificial intelligence (AI) and the VUCA conditions of global landscapes, EI skills are more critical today than ever. The proliferation of AI can cause EI skills to fade while the VUCA landscape calls for adept interpersonal skills—social skills are at a premium. Both skills fade, and enhanced social skills can be addressed through a coaching organization by reinforcing the EI skills through its inherent structure of hands-on engagements. EI consists of five components—self-awareness, self-regulation, motivation, empathy, and social skill. The first three core competences are intrapersonal or self-management skills while the latter two are interpersonal or a person's ability to manage relationships with others.[68]

The core competences of EI coupled with assessments help leadership coaches evaluate themselves and identify/link with their coachees. The social components serve as barometers for determining the coach's ability to judge the distance to the coachee. Furthermore, they predispose how well one can adjust to the dynamics associated with working amid disparate cultures.[69] These two social behavioral components will be further explored in chapters 4 and 5 as they are essential components and key enablers for *coaching triangulation*. They determine the coach's capacity to navigate blind spots and demonstrate coaching efficacy in a coaching conversation.

This chapter illustrates how the five components of EI are pivotal to fixing the coach's position, so she/he can identify with where she/he is in relation to the aspiring leader.[70] It defines these five components and illustrates how they influence the behavior of leadership coaches. Moreover, this chapter explores how the EI components work interdependently to clearly fix the location of the leadership coach. They enable the coach to reach the coachee through self-awareness. To expand on the interdependencies of the EI coach and coachee, assessments are administered to refine their position and their overall disposition to determine their relative locations with regards to their personal strengths and weaknesses. EI and assessments represent the foundation of the leadership coaching platform, providing the fundamental mechanisms to underpin the coach's aptitude to identify his/her individual perspective and link it to that of the coachee.

In the same spirit of asking whether leaders are born or made, can EI components be learned and enhanced?[71] This question suggests considering dependencies and interdependencies of each component and their relationship with self-assessments and individual values (which will be further explored in chapter 4). In addition to locating and judging the distance to the aspiring leader, a coach must have the capacity to cultivate a viable path for the coachee to become his successor. Moreover, assessments serve as a nexus to link both the leader and aspiring leader. In addition to locating aspiring leaders, these components and inherent skills revealed through assessments are key to gauging the disposition and coaching amid disparate cultures.

> *Leaders must make organizational decisions with the best interest of the individual who make up the organization in mind—they must mentor and build...build the bench and prepare the bench to lead.*
> —Jason M. Jones, Esq. (January 16, 2022, Zoom call)

Leadership development should be based on the coach's awareness of his/her current position, or better yet EI prowess, coupled with a commitment to develop aspiring leaders.[72] This awareness, in turn, dictates and informs the methodology which is most appropriate to oversee leadership programs in organizations. I use the term certain organization because organizations are baselined on foundational and core principles. For example, implementing a leadership program in a heterogenous culture requires stronger EI as opposed to a homogeneous culture where everyone shares similar views on leadership development. Heterogeneous landscape requires formalized processes to shape actions and initiate leadership development. The key to effective leadership development is establishing a baseline because leadership development is a learning continuum.

From the perspective of leadership theory, Peter Northouse limited the EI and leadership association to traits, skills, and style with each consisting of interchangeable parts and mutually dependable attributes.[73] I would link social intelligence with both skills and EI while arguing that social intelligence is predicated on EI. I would submit that social intelligence and EI are mutually inclusive in that they both determine how the coach relates to the coachee. Because leadership coaches possess varying levels of EI, leadership coaching is scalable. However, enhancing EI components enables coaches the requisite flexibility to adapt to multifaceted environments and excel in diverse landscapes. This flexibility affords leadership coaches more maneuver space for determining their position and, moreover, their relative position to the coachee. Perhaps, increased EI allows them to occupy the same space as the coachee. This flexibility could manifest, cultivating a more viable and symmetrical path to success for the coach, coachee, and organization holistically.

Finally, leadership coaching can be illustrated in various forms, but it eventually distills down to how capable a leader is at influencing an aspiring leader.[74] This influence is dependent on judging the distance between the coach and coachee whereas the first marker is the leader's location, which is predicated on his/her five components of EI and self-assessments.

Five components of EI

When leading in dynamic global landscapes, leadership coaches with a high degree of EI have proven to be the most effective.[75] Also, managers who strive to improve the EI of self and that of their aspiring leaders will decrease their organizational turnover and decrease the costs of recruitment, training, and adaptation of the new human assets.[76] This resonates well with coaching, as not only does it apply EI to adapt to disparate cultures, it also provides a viable platform for improving EI skills by personifying a learning process for both the coach and coachee. The capacity to build self-awareness, to self-regulate, motivate, demonstrate empathy, and apply interpersonal skills are paramount to leadership coaching as they define the coach's position and are also catalyst to his/her ability to appreciate the coachee's location. Table 4a provides the definition and hallmarks of the components of EI.[77]

The Five Components of EI at Work			
	Definition	Hallmarks	ICF Core Competency
Self-Awareness	Recognizing and understanding moods, emotions, and drives, and their effects on others	-Self-confidence -Realistic self-assessment -Self-deprecating sense of humor	Understanding the fit for coaching relationship
Self-Regulation	- Ability to control or redirect impulses and moods - The propensity to suspend judgment; thinking before acting.	-Trustworthiness and integrity - Comfort with ambiguity - Openness to change	- Confidently shifts perspective - Allows client to vent situation without judgment - Open to adjusting behaviors and actions regarding coaching plan
Motivation	- Passion for work not driven by money or status - Propensity to pursue goals with energy and persistence	- Strong drive to achieve - Optimism even when facing failure - Organizational commitment	- Uses humor effectively to create lightness and energy - Positively confronts client to move on agreed-upon actions
Empathy	- Ability to understand the emotional makeup of other people - Adroit at treating people according to their emotional reaction	- Expertise in building and retaining talent - Cross-cultural sensitivity - Service to client and customers	- Active listening and understanding client's perspective - Senses client's concern
Interpersonal Skills	- Proficient managing relationships and building networks - Able to find common ground and build rapport	- Effective in leading change - Persuasive - Expert in building and leading teams	- Provokes new ideas - Keeps coachee on track according to prescribed improvement plan

Table 4a. The five components of EI at work

Self-awareness: Foundational/enabling component

Self-awareness is the first and enabling component of EI as it personifies knowing oneself by embodying a deep understanding of emotions, strengths, weaknesses, needs, and motives.[78] This personal attribute surrounds self-honesty that hinges on self-confidence, which engenders openness. Furthermore, self-awareness extends to a person keenly understanding how his/her values and goals serve as a barometer to the capacity to self-assess. This EI component represents both the foundation and springboard for the four associated components. It is critical to leadership coaching because it helps the coach self-assess, which is vital to marking the coach's location to enable *coaching triangulation.*

Self-awareness is also pivotal to the coach's capacity to navigate blind spots. Coaches with a high degree of self-awareness are in tune with how feelings influence the behavior of those she/he supports and helps improve on their job performance, which, in turn, affects the organizational environment.[79] This component also supports facilitating and learning when performing career-championing imperatives, such as intermediate performance reviews (IPRs). Self-aware individuals are confident when discussing their limitations and strengths and are eager for feedback to inform course adjustments; they welcome constructive criticism.[80] Please refer to chapter 8 for IPRs and their impact on organizational wellness.

Self-regulation: Actionable component

Self-regulation is the actionable component that enables self-awareness that leads to the realization of the need to manage behavior. Self-regulation is the toughest skill to get one's head around because it deals with the biological impulses that drive emotions that requires constant behavior adjustment and conscious effort in self-management.[81] Actually, self-management would be a more appropriate term for this EI component as emotions are managed through conscientious efforts that can be enhanced with leadership development. Self-regulation is integral to establishing an environments of trust and fairness and excelling amid VUCA conditions as both are dependent on people who can manage their feelings and impulses and master their emotions.[82] General Electric's leadership model is comprised of four *E*s, which are energy, energize, edge, and execute.[83] To that end, I associate this component with what Jack Welch refers to as having the "edge" to make difficult decisions as mastering emotions must be intentional.[84] Some of the smartest people experienced difficulties making tough yes-or-no decisions.[85] I relate this to making decisions on whether to act under pressurized conditions.

As I reflect on my career and ponder the biggest challenges of today, I would submit self-regulation is the skill I find most elusive. Exuding self-awareness can manifest without embodying the capacity to resist temptations to act. I do a good job understanding my surroundings but find self-management more challenging during less desirable circumstances. These situations require me to develop a level deeper to manage my natural impulses or passion toward situations. As well, I can attest to this experience firsthand as I look back at my EQ-i assessment; my lower score was in impulse control. The irony is people of fiery temperament are thought of as being passionate and charismatic until they reach higher levels of responsibility and it begins to work against them.[86] The bottom line is understanding and managing oneself is just as important, if not more critical, than managing those which one encounters. This skill is pivotal in VUCA environments, owing to its hallmark of being open to change.

Motivation: Dynamic component

This is a dynamic component that dictates the rate or intensity, or better yet viability, of action steps. If I was not already utterly passionate about leadership coaching, just the mere thought of this trait's hallmarks gets me even more amped up. Motivation trait brings unprecedented, naturally embedded excitement because it strikes an internal cord that I have consistently applied to create success in organizations which whom I was affiliated. It is my conviction anyone in a leadership position should be committed to encourage their understudies to achieve beyond expectations; doing so should be an honor. Leadership coaches who exemplify this trait have an embedded desire to seek out creative challenges, are enamored by learning, and take pride in a job well done.[87] These leaders are infectious throughout organizations. This skills underscores leading by example by modeling the way.

To borrow insight once again from GE four *E*s, this component pivots on energy and energize, which are having energy and the capacity to energize others, respectively.[88] Specifically, energy and energize resonate in the motivation component as they are associated with the ability to exhibit motivation and capacity to extract greatness from those whom one encounters. These types of leaders naturally seek improvement or pursue ways and opportunities to do things better.[89] In parallel to coaching having an impact on the coach, coachee, and organization, people who are naturally driven to do better track the progress of self, their team, and the organization.[90] Finally, in the same fashion *coaching triangulation* yields a succession plan for leadership, coaches who embody the motivation trait builds a team of managers around themselves with the same traits where optimism and organizational commitment are fundamental to embedded leadership practices.[91]

Empathy: Game changing component—a coaching conversation enabler

Everyone is an individual and must be understood for who they are rather than who leaders perceive them to be. Empathy is the EI component that bridges the gap. According to *Webster*, empathy is the action of understanding, being aware of, being sensitive to, and vicariously experiencing the feelings, thoughts, and experience of another of either past or present without having the feelings, thoughts, and experience fully communicated in an objectively *explicit* manner. Is it possible for someone to exhibit empathy toward an individual for which she/he lacks the wherewithal to garner or share a common perspective? Empathy is a pivotal EI component because it allows leaders to work with aspiring leaders from their respective locations.

Empathy is particularly important to current landscapes because it promotes teamwork, connects disparate groups, and helps to retain talent.[92] This skill comprises the wherewithal to understand the importance of speaking with others on their level and from their respective, regardless of background differences. This level of understanding entails delving into the meaning behind what the coachee is conveying for a deeper learning experience.[93] Unearthing this knowledge better equips the coach to facilitate the aspiring leader's learning and development and move him/her along successful paths. Empathy fosters trust and engenders the interpersonal relationship between the coach and coachee. Hence, it helps the coach move the coachee through engaging based on individual needs.[94]

Empathy, more so than any other EI component, is the key to leading across disparate cultures as it allows leadership coaches to ingratiate across all groups, hence suppressing in-group favoritism. This EI component is essential to suppressing blind spots by identifying with others as will be explained in chapter 4. Conversely, failure to demonstrate empathy could create an untrusting relationship and the proclivity to be critical toward others.[95] Empathy is the antidote for eradicating potential miscues and misunderstandings which emanate from cross-cultural dialogue.

Interpersonal skills: All-encompassing component

> *When coaching, you must not only care about people, but you also need people skills.*
> —Anthony Simmons

Of the five components of EI, this one is most fitting for the question of whether these skills are innate or developed. Regardless, this component is essential as it is considered the culmination of EI components. Not only does it involve the capacity to motivate and energize others, but it also portends possessing the skills to execute. To borrow GE's fourth E, the capacity to get the job done.[96] This skill is pivotal in diverse environments because people with keen social skills have a natural knack for finding common ground with people of all kinds.[97]

Owing to its openness to new ideas, this skill is unique to leadership coaches and their propensity to identify talent, motivate employees, and facilitate challenging assignments to foster growth and development through continued learning.[98] Team building and interpersonal skills work together in organizations as interpersonal skills are pivotal to executive program managers in dealing effectively with those whom they lead by being cognizant of their leadership development needs.[99] It is important to note EI is important for the coach based on his/her expertise and ability to understand the EI of clients; therefore, it is used to both identify the coach's perspective and assist the coach in relating to the coachee's position.[100]

Notwithstanding, assessments are performed on both the coach and coachee as a nexus for relative positions or linking their positions. EI and assessments are pivotal to the *coaching triangulation* model. If I had to rotate the triangle, I would pivot it on this position/point as it would represent the fulcrum for the process.

Self-assessments

The question of whether leaders are born or made is commonplace—perhaps the answer dwells in assessment results as they determine where one is on the EI scale. As for myself, considering my journey in leadership positions since my formative years as a student-athlete and the results from my assessment, I would humbly label myself as a born leader. In the same spirit and on accord with my leadership-coaching thesis, a second-order question occurs: whether leadership coaches are born or developed. Based on results from myriad assessments and hands-on coaching experiences, I would submit coaches are always learning and developing new attributes.

Notwithstanding, self-analysis allows you to understand yourself so you can have a chance to understand others and filter information to understand your surroundings whether immediate or global. As a result, self-analysis instruments lead to prudence in decision-making. Assessments are key to baselining individual coaching engagements.[101] As well, talent management in organizations across borders requires assessments of the respective leaders' global leadership competencies.[102] Assessments accentuate coaching relationships because they afford coaches self-awareness of themselves so they can adequately apply their strengths effectively. In addition to providing a valid profile on individual strengths, assessments unearth unrealized talents coaches embody.[103] More importantly, assessments confirm and solidify attributes that would otherwise act as ethical blind spots—gaps between who coaches are and who they think they are—to which the thesis of this work aims to ameliorate.[104] Though knowing oneself is important for coaching, assessments are invaluable when working across disparate cultures in global expanses as they fix the location of the coach against the disposition of other cultures.

Is it possible to know whether the coach and coachee are on the right course if they are unaware of their current position? What does assessments portend? Assessments help fix locations and facilitate the cross-pollination of the leader and aspiring leader. Conducting an assessment is akin to fixing one's position with a GPS in that it helps both the coach and coachee determine their current position to decide which course is appropriate to move in synchronization. First, locations must be established before designing a viable course for success. These assessments are key to understanding where one is in relation to strengths and weaknesses as leadership coaches are only as effective as they are in tune with their strengths and weaknesses.[105] It behooves the coach and coachee to apply the same assessment tool as a barometer to mark their relative dispositions. Also, assessments even add more value when combined across difference tools and integrated with EI components.

Not only are assessments coaching imperatives to mark the coach and coachee positions, but they are also pivotal in global landscapes because they allow coaches to align skills to leadership applications based on cultures. Communities function best when they are built around people areas of competence.[106] Furthermore, assessments facilitate authentic relationships that stem from transparency as opposed to how matters appear.[107] The coach and coachee are connected by using assessment tools to identify disconnects and common ground to determine the degree of engagement necessitated to mark the start point for navigating blind spots and getting to a viable coaching conversation. This mark is based on both EI capacity and self-assessments results.

What is the correlation between EI components and self-assessments? It could be argued that the components of EI enable self-assessments whereas self-awareness generates openness. Are assessments shaped by the components of EI? Can someone self-assess if they lack self-awareness? Does self-confidence underscore an honest self-assessment? Does self-actualization enable this condition? Spoken differently, does an individual have to feel accomplished to be transparent? Regardless of the leader's leadership competence level, the assessment accuracy and development capacity hinge on the leader's humble spirits that encompass transparency, identifying with their weaknesses, and refraining from making excuses.[108]

Assessments afford the leader a baseline where she/he may stand on interpersonal skills with respect to the client. Essentially, it provides the connection between the coach and coachee based on their respective dispositions. To that point, these tools should be applied at the outset of relationship to help baseline the coach-and-coachee perspectives on management and due processes. For example, the Navy administers the Myers-Briggs Type Indicator (MBTI) at executive leadership courses, and they are often administered when deciding on fits for key, mostly executive staff positions. This is critical to determine the fit between executives and their assistants. Nonetheless, owing to the nature and spirit of coaching, assessments should never occur in reaction. Rather assessments should be deliberate while aiming to foster amicable relationships between the coach and coachee to address lingering and sensitive issues in a constructive atmosphere.[109]

The most accurate way to fix the location of the coach and coachee is to use different types of assessments and compare the results. In my experience, although I have taken myriad self-assessments, I deemed the MBTI, EQ-i, Gallup's Clifton StrengthsFinder, and spiritual gifts assessments as most appropriate to inform the intent of this work as they afford common components to support integrative results. When comparing the result I garnered for these separate tools, I discovered undue synergy between my strengths and weaknesses as they relate my coaching aptitude. As stated earlier, it is paramount for the coach to determine the relative location to the coachee by comparing his/her results to that of the coachee. Coaches should aspire to meet the coachees halfway. Assessments are a must for identifying the halfway point whether emotionally, socially, ethnically, generationally, and so forth. The following subparagraphs highlights the four tools that I have found invaluable.

MBTI

The MBTI is a viable tool for gauging how people behave as the psychodynamic approach to leadership coaching values personality as the intrinsic fabric of personal thinking, feelings, and acting with regard to people and their respective environments.[110] This assessment is normally applied before the onset of the coaching session as it offers an open book of who I am to set the stage for an energizing and full engagement. Performing an assessment before the first meeting serves as a baseline for the first coaching session by establishing a foundation while encouraging the cocreating of relationships between the coach and coachee as prescribed in the first two clusters of the ICF core competencies and CCNI (coachfederation.org/core-competencies and_https://christiancoaches.com/wp-content/uploads/2017/10/Competencies-Edited-Final-2017.pdf). My personal preferences are more introverted, sensing, thinking, and judging as opposed to extroverted, intuitive, feeling, and perceptive respectively. Extroverted (open-minded) and agreeable leaders are more inclined to foster relationships and accommodate people.[111]

What are the implications of MBTI and EQ-i regarding interpersonal skills? Do the traits associated with these tools drive behavior toward dealing with people? Do intuitive feelers struggle with people skills? My MBTI results are ISTJ, whose preferences are typically for the dependable, realistic, and practical. ISTJs remember and use facts and want things clearly and logically stated. They tend to be thorough, systematic, hardworking, and careful with particulars and procedures. When they anticipate things need to be done, they don't hesitate to take on responsibilities. Once involved, ISTJs are committed and hard to distract and discourage—they lend stability to projects and persevere in the face of adversity. These results parallel my approach to organizational leadership and have been the fulcrum to my success at achieving OW during my four positions as a chief executive. However, my sensing included an out-of-preference mark when comparing practical and conceptual. Though this registered as an anomaly on the MBTI, it matched my Clifton's top five as an intellection as conceptual entails scholarly, idea-oriented, and intellectual. My adeptness to recognize situations and take immediate action while assisting team members is in concert with my motivational gifts as a perceiver and teacher. Perceivers and teachers thrive on full engagement as they thrive on being physically energized, emotionally connected, mentally focused, and spiritually aligned with a purpose that exceeds self-interest. [112]

EMOTIONAL INTELLIGENCE AND ASSESSMENTS
REALIZE LOCATIONS FOR COACH AND COACHEE

In the same vein that assessments are used to determine relative location between coachee and coachees, mentors and career advisors have consistently instructed me to inquire about my bosses' or executives' MBTI preferences during the onboarding process. Specifically, this tool is leveraged for strategic placement and assignment of sought-after positions. This assessment should not occur as a onetime endeavor, rather it should be taken periodically, during career milestones, and at the outset of increased responsibilities, and it should be aligned with expanded/senior leadership courses. This assertion is based on the premise that strengths do change with time especially under demanding coaching needs and varying job requirements. This behavior became evident during my tenure at the pentagon as my sensible trait changed to intuitive. I attributed this change to the austere acquisition and budgeting environment when intuitive reasoning triumphed sensible recourse to acquiring war-fighting systems.

EQ-i

How emotional intelligent are you, and are you aware of how much the scores from this report drive your five components of EI? How good do you feel about yourself as a professional? This assessment tool consists of results for total EQ, five composite scales, and fifteen subscales. Any score above one hundred indicates enhanced emotional functioning while scores less than one hundred indicate areas which may be improved; EI components with higher scores are associated with higher levels of EI and better performance.[113]

I took the EQ-i assessment as part of my professional/executive development as a senior Naval officer. However, when comparing my results to the hallmarks of EI components, I immediately noticed I had committed/experienced a colossal oversight on impulse-control score. The score was well below average. The oversight was I failed to address the matter to improve my EI component of self-regulation. The irony is I have been contemplating and struggling with trying to improve in this area over the past several years, not being aware that this shortcoming was brought to my attention nearly ten years ago. I share this story to encourage coaches and aspiring leaders alike to assess and take measure to address the blind spots discovered in the assessment.

Motivational gift test

The motivational gifts were assessed using DellaVecchio's assessment tool, which examines the Roman's chapter 12 gifts to perceive, serve, teach, encourage, give, rule, show mercy. My top gifts are my ability to perceive and teach. These God-given gifts underscore my passion for leadership coaching and substantiates my appropriateness for sharing my insights through this book; coaching draws out the abilities God blesses one with.[114] To codify these gifts, I cross-walked my spiritual gifts with the EI hallmarks of self-awareness and self-regulation as perceiving allows me to discern circles of influence and circles of concern while teaching increases the former circle and decreases the latter. The circle of influence (manageable) should be as large as possible, and the circle of concern (unmanageable) should be minuscule. [115]

Having already considered myself a natural leader—based on personal insights gleaned from myriad leadership courses and hands-on experiences—I was not surprised to discover my motivational gifts reflected a coaching pedigree. Coaches are transformational and natural teachers while teaching is transformational as it develops people and the process for achieving results.[116] Teachers are passionate about their convictions to the point where they can appear argumentative while attempting to gain clarification.[117] I do not sway from this approach when I am making a compelling argument or attempting to imbue constituents with valuable lessons. Teachers are savvy in their techniques when it comes to imbuing constituents with knowledge as they can act as consummate debaters if they deem this approach as necessary to help others to learn.[118] As well, teachers are gifted in making difficult concepts appear easy to understand.[119] Their motivation is to help others learn and grow by presenting truth in a logical way. Teachers tend to be gifted intellectually and often seek to become experts in their fields.[120] Teachers are usually comfortable addressing large groups. These characteristics are direct reflections of my passion to translate difficult concepts into user-friendly, actionable concepts. As well, I feel it is essential for leaders to exhibit a high level of intellectual capabilities and exude expertise in his/her field of involvement.[121]

As a perceiver, my keen sense of discerning between what is right and wrong aligns to my proclivity to immediately identify unwanted behaviors or disruptive activities. The gift affords one the extraordinary ability to discern and proclaim truth.[122] Navy executives often refer to this extraordinary ability as the little voice in the back of commanding officers' head that enables him/her to get ahead of or ward off perceived chaos—it behooves commanding officers to have this gift at their disposal. From a firsthand perspective, I would unequivocally say that my gift of perceiving afforded me the ability to trust and follow that voice when I sensed that things were not quite right.

My leadership style of ruler aligns with my inclination to pride myself on leading by example and observing structured processes. Just as rulers bring order by setting up structures, systems, and methods for others to follow, I am keen on systemic methodologies to establishing consistent work environments which are based on my *"main thing"* which will be presented in chapter 8. Also, rulers have an ability to capture the "big picture" and anticipate the proclivity for unwanted conditions and outcomes. Rulers are galvanizers which requires strong interpersonal skills to guide everyone toward a common goal. Hence, rulers are protectors with an assertive, take-charge approach that, at times, can cause rulers to appear bossy to other people who do not understand the gift.[123]

The next highest spiritual gift was to show mercy which has parallelism with EI attribute of empathy. This gift entails having an extraordinary ability to feel and act upon genuine empathy for others who are faced with inequities and distressing physical, mental, emotional, social, and spiritual pains.[124] These gifts lend to my vehement approach toward implementing a talent management process to catapult organizational success which will be illustrated in coach-protégé and IPRs initiatives in chapter 8.

Clifton StrengthsFinder

> *I discovered my Clifton Strengths, and it has changed my life. I am more aware of how I feel and act in different situations, and I better understand why others act as they do. I use this assessment tool to help people be the best version of themselves and succeed.*
> —Hildur BergÞorsdottir, People
> Analytics Specialist, Icelandair

Based on Gallup's research, there are four distinct domains of leadership: executing, influencing, relationship building, and strategic thinking. My Clifton StrengthsFinder top five strengths are (1) responsibility, (2) learner, (3) achiever, (4) intellection, and (5) focus. Of these four domains, I have three strengths in the executing and two in the strategic-thinking domains. Ideally, one would prefer to have a strength in all four domains for well-roundedness; however, this domain gap is complemented by a well-rounded team. The StrengthsFinder tool adds unique value in determining how team members can maximize their contribution to team's collective goals.[125] Moreover, for leadership coaching amid disparate groups, the StrengthsFinder assessments allow coaches to identify competencies to strategically position assets amid unfamiliar and varying global terrains. Understanding and comparing your StrengthsFinder top five with other tools can add more value to assessments by identifying where each team member stands and can contribute to team building amid disparate groups. Having three of my top five in the execution domain is well in alignment with my MBTI results and confirms my strength to get things done timely.[126]

In summary, measuring EI prowess and performing self-assessments are critical steps to navigating blind spots because each helps coaches recognize the existence of potential leadership impediments. However, coaching can bolster EI, which, in turn, engenders emotional maturity which is one of the key factors to a leader's capacity to suppress these blind spots. This process entails garnering the wherewithal to best assess where coaches are on social and behavior intelligence, self-management skills, and interrelation acumen. The capacity to suppress blind spots sets the precedent for the initial link/connection between the coach and coachee; both rely on this measure to mark the jump-off point of the coaching relationship to, henceforth, inform the coaching conversation.

Once the location is recognized, navigating blind spots enables the coaching conversation by removing barriers that would otherwise preclude the coach from considering the aspiring leader's disposition. In essence, the culmination of this chapter sets the stage for the next two chapters, making for a viable coaching conversation where ethical biases are suppressed to facilitate an open dialogue to measure self-awareness from a mutual vantage point. If the hypothesis that EI components and the four assessment tools I have been administered and presented in this chapter are interrelated, leadership coaches are afforded an entering argument to gauge the path and identify the challenges associated with navigating blind spots. The literature illustrated in chapter 4 is germane to further this thesis.

Navigating Blind Spots for Renewed Vision to Judge Distance to Coachees

Blind spots exist in the gap between intended and actual ethical behavior, the person you want to be and the person you are.[127] Navigating these gaps affords leadership coaches a renewed vision to judge the distance to aspiring leaders. Because of sacrosanct cultural beliefs, ethical behaviors, values scarcity, and generational gaps, it is inevitable for blind spots to manifest across global organizations. These blind spots contribute to the fundamental attribution error where leaders fail to relate to constituents' situations and conditions.[128] These attribution errors must be addressed to identify the relative position between the coach and coachee. This feat is achieved by removing blind spots to shed new light on the leader and aspiring leader's location.

Navigating blind spots allows coaches to judge the relative distance between him/her and the coachee. Getting to know people is critical, but getting to know them from their cultural vantage point is even more critical. Considering the virtual world that we live in today. There is an increased propensity to interact with people of diverse cultures; therefore, it is imperative to identify with respective locations. It would be hard to imagine anyone in a coaching position who would not want to serve the best interests of everyone in the organization. However, the problem is there are too many individuals in key leadership positions who possess low levels of self-awareness. This anemic self-awareness warrants a renewed vision to gain insight into the viewpoint of disparate groups. This insight removes the adverse behaviors associated with managing across disparate groups: in-groups and out-groups are homogenized.

This chapter addresses EI and values, generational disparities, cultural implications, and leadership ethics across disparate groups and illustrates how blind spots are navigated by understanding and ameliorating the conditions associated with diverse groups in global landscapes. It discusses the roles of culture and values amid diverse groups, how ethics and generational disparities can adversely impact thinking and cloud decisions amid disparate groups. These varying perspectives are what generate blind spots. Accordingly, the thesis unearths how beliefs, values, and ethics influence the behaviors inside organizations and the underlying actors that emanate these behaviors. It affords scholarly insight on how to navigate blind spots by aligning values, behavioral ethics, generations, and cultures with doing what's right. The chapter explores how coaches can have discernment regarding deontology—the want-to-self versus the ought-to-self [129] or better yet what one should do against what one wants to do.[130] Finally, it provides remedies to suppress unwanted ethical behaviors to realize a common lens to coach in diverse landscapes.

What causes blind spots? How they are impacted by values? Must one have a solid core of values, behavioral ethics, and individual perspective to do what's right? How does one overcome personal beliefs that were instilled during her/his formative years? Blind spots are like the unconscious in that they are everything a person doesn't know or can't observe within themself. Navigating blind spots is putting the interest or betterment of the next person before self. Not only does this measure help leaders right themselves, but it also helps them to understand how they developed these leadership barriers. Furthermore, navigating blind spots helps to enjoy a renewed perspective of the aspiring leader by removing restraints caused by personal views which stem from learned behaviors. However, the flawed human approach to ethical decisions which oftentimes can be either egotistic or culturally biased, get in the way.[131] Suppressing blind spots affords leadership coaches the wherewithal to normalize behaviors toward in-groups and out-groups. In-groups are those for which one has more in common while out-groups are the antithesis.

Although this work focuses on leading diverse cultures amid global landscapes, coaches must first master individual domains— themselves. If EI and self-assessment help coaches determine where they are and identify with the location of coachees, then navigating blind spots enables the coach to share a common space with the coachee. They must be adept at overcoming biases associated with personal values and beliefs and ethical and cultural disparities. Coaches must understand where they are socially, emotionally, spiritually, and professionally. Then they must understand the location of those they aim to reach before helping them design a path for growth and development. They must be keen on determining how all parties must maneuver to mitigate obstacles.

Vignette: The most pressing leadership issues of today

Today's outlook on leadership is highlighted by two challenges: (1) too many leadership positions are occupied by people who are not emotionally and socially qualified to lead and (2) the "Information Age" has manifested an environment where people lack basic life skills.

As for too many leadership positions being occupied by nonqualified individuals, it is my assertion that there is a systemic problem in youth sports, schools, churches, military, and corporate organizations where the appointed person advocates for himself at the peril of his subordinates. Most effective leaders are alike in that they have a high degree of emotional intelligence—self-awareness, self-regulation, motivation, empathy, and social skill.[132] Many leaders of today lack the self-awareness, self-regulation, and social skill to positively influence followers. The aplomb of high-caliber leaders has yielded to the whim and willingness of less-capable leaders. The latter is willing to do whatever it takes to ascend the ranks while the former is unwilling to compromise standards and values for promotion. It is akin to David versus Goliath; the gifted takes his talents for granted while the inferior relentlessly pursues ways to excel—he takes on increased tasks and aligns himself with decision makers to advance his cause. This has resulted in leadership positions being occupied by individuals who tend to actualize through subordinates.

The second issue surrounds the mere fact that people are isolated and independent while immersing themselves into information tools rather than interacting personally. Personal interaction facilitates cognitive development, renewal, and enhancement. Social cognition is the way we (human beings) interpret, analyze, and remember information about the social world.[133] To effectively lead, one must understand the basics about social cognition. People must make a concerted effort to overcome the tendency to go it alone!

Whether performing research efforts, organizational training, or venturing into entertainment opportunities and venues, people are inclined or resolved to act independently. This ostensibly hampers cognitive development and sustainment, which ultimately erodes life skills. Regardless of how technologically advanced the world becomes, there will always be a requirement for human interactions. The skills that enable human interaction must not only be developed, but also, there will always be a demand for them to be refined. This feat is only possible through practice and a renewed emphasis on reinforcing basic communication skills, such as eye contact, tone of voice, and body language.

In summary, the confluence of selfish leaders and social ineptitude will strangle our youth, communities, churches, government entities, and industry. Leaders must be self-assured, and people must interact to develop and refine their social skills.

EI and values interdependencies

Too often leaders ascend to positions for which they are uncomfortable executing or performing at, so they resort to questionable practices to sustain their positions (Dr. R. Lee, personal communication, January 12, 2022). If learning how important EI is to coach disparate groups in global landscapes in the previous chapter was not convincing, exploring the interrelations between EI and values in this chapter should be utterly captivating. Individuals have personal beliefs about what is important in life that personify their values. Understanding values requires one to appreciate the relationship between values and personal needs.[134] People have basic (foundational) needs (physiological, safety, and social) and higher-level (progressive) needs (esteem, and self-actualization). The basic needs are the basis for higher-level needs.[135] The basic needs are reflected in values of survival, safety, and belonging, self-esteem, and personal growth.[136] The first three needs are associated with defensive behavior while the latter two are of higher order as they relate to growth and development to support a higher state of being. The irony regarding coaching leadership is basic needs provide the foundation for the higher-level needs; therefore, individuals who have not fulfilled the need for security lack the basis to strive at developing others, owing to lack of esteem and self-actualization. If basic needs are not satisfied, a dilemma ensues that places the coach between a choice of pulling toward safety and pushing for growth and development.[137] To develop others, leaders must have experienced a transition from basic needs (limited to transactional behavior) to higher-order needs (enable transformational skills) as depicted in Figure 4a.[138]

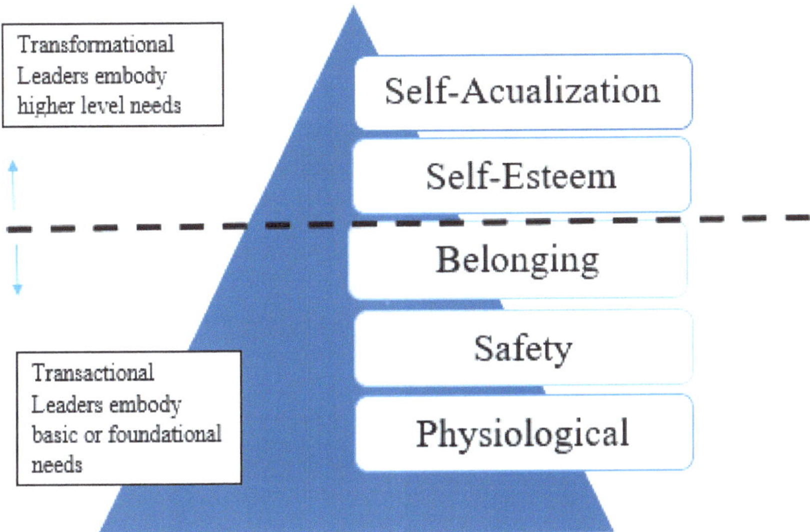

Figure 4a. Needs vs. leadership capacity

Leaders who have not experienced progression lack the capacity to transform others as they are too frail because they are defensive and less inclined to accept negative reinforcement. Moreover, not attaining foundational needs oftentimes results in individuals occupying leadership positions only to stand on the shoulders of a coachee who is not capable of holding them up. I refer to this condition as upside-down leadership. In parallel with coaches knowing their location to identify with the location of coachee, it is my conviction that leadership coaches will lack the aptitude/capacity to develop new coaches if they have not experienced personal growth or higher-order needs development. Absent of this development, people continuously seek security and exhibit a defensive demeanor rather than leading objectively.[139]

Values and social identity

Values are principles or standards you must acquire to prepare yourself for life's walk. Social identity encompasses the construct of individuals based on culture and beliefs, values, and norms that shape character traits.[140] With regard to social identify, coaching has a direct dependency on how one leverages her/his character traits. These traits baseline an individual's coaching prowess or location.[141] In that spirit, engaging in team building and coaching requires one to first maximize intrapersonal capabilities, such as trustworthiness, positive attitude, dependability, and adaptability.[142] These intrapersonal skills are dependent on where a person is on life's needs curve by way of values obtained as an individual's level of personal development has a direct impact on his/her outlook on life.

A shared culture of individual values is based on how individuals select values to obtain the things they find to be important in life. Values fall in three categories: espoused, actual, and desired. Espoused values are the ones people say they value, actual values guide current behavior, and desired values are ones that individuals would like to have to guide behavior.[143] Basically, personal values are a function of what an individual has done to position her/himself for success or have prepared to pursue and realize goals (terminal values) envisioned.

Distinguishing values address two questions: "What does one want to achieve?" and "How does one want to achieve it?"[144] Values are distinguished between terminal values (world peace, wisdom, and happiness), which are the preferred end state of existence and instrumental values (responsibility, cooperation, and customer service), which are preferred modes of conduct.[145] Values are also associated with end states in that a specific end state of existence is personally or socially preferable to the converse end state of existence.[146] Stated slightly differently, values center around a person's internal psychological makeup, whereas terminal values are the end state that someone desires in life, and instrumental values are the means to achieve that desired end state.[147] At the personal level, values surround an individual's beliefs about what is important to substantiate life (ends) and the principles (means) applied to attain this status.[148] Table 5a provides some common instrumental values that enable terminal values (goals and vision). These values are key and essential to meeting individual needs and requisite skills for becoming an executive leadership coach and effectively leading in diverse cultures.[149]

Instrumental Values	Terminal Values
Honesty	Increased Productivity
Ambition	Growth
Dependability	Expanded Mission
Creativity	Diversification
Competence	Financial Growth
Enthusiasm	Improve Efficiencies
Self-Discipline	Increased Profits
Capable Workforce	Equality
Authenticity	Sense of Accomplishment
Commitment	Wisdom
Self-Assurance	Trust
Openness to Change	Authentic Relationships
Humility	Security
Courageous	Recognition
Interpersonal Skills	Freedom
Adaptability	Authority
Communications	Self-Efficacy

Table 5a. Instrumental and terminal values

Authentic and ethical leaders foster environments of trust, virtuousness, and transparency and do not compromise their values. They value whatever is in the best interest of the company.[150] These leaders know the right thing to do under difficult circumstances. They use challenging situations to strengthen their values as values represent what is good, bad, or important to the company.[151] When considering values, it is noteworthy to discern the three cultural layers: artifacts, espoused values, and basic underlying assumptions. Whereas artifacts (things we see, hear, and feel) are the first cultural layer, the second and third layers are espoused values (what ought to be based on rationalization and unconscious desires) and basic underlying assumptions (taken-for-granted beliefs and ideals) respectively.[152] Chapter 6 provides a detailed explanation of the three layers of culture.

Coaching across generations

Considering the workforce consists of five generations—Traditionalist (1928–1945); baby boomers (1946–1964); Generation X (1965–1980); Generation Y (1981–1996); and Generation Z (1997–2015)—organizational leaders must be mindful of each generation's values and differences for performance efficacy.[153] To capitalize on these diverse attributes, it is incumbent on coaches to implement an environment of shared values through collaboration that is realized through fostering trust and facilitating relationships.[154] Considering these conditions, leaders must carefully assess generational barriers if they are to effectively facilitate relationships and build trust. Coaches must be made aware of the differences in attitudes and opinions as they relate to organizational standards.[155]

Common behaviors across generations must be assessed to understand how to build the relationships of trust required to facilitate an environment of shared values. When coaching across five generation in VUCA environments, it is prudent to assume communications, and associated interpersonal skills will vary vastly. Couple this with the prospect of immediate gratification and propensity for immediate empowerment by the newer generations, coaches must devise means for managing with due regard for generational particularities as it can be an extremely demanding process. Leadership styles must be adjusted to enable a new shared culture.[156]

Culture implications

In Western languages, culture means refinement of the mind with education, art, and literature, whereas one's mental programs lie within the social environment experienced when growing up: family, neighborhood, school, youth groups, workplace, and living community.[157] Every person carries within himself/herself patterns of thinking, feeling, and acting which stemmed from a lifetime of learned behaviors.[158] Culture is the accumulated shared learning surrounding beliefs, values, and behavioral norms regarding the following categories: observed behavioral regularities when people interact; climate; formal rituals and celebrations; formal philosophy; group norms; rules of the game; identity and images of self; habits of thinking;

mental models; linguistic paradigms; shared meanings; and root metaphors or integrating symbols.[159] From a culture perspective, blind spots are the difference between how you think you act toward cultures and what the coachee sees from his/her vantage point.[160]

Organizations don't possess values. But organizational culture is shaped by the values of the individuals who set the boundaries in which organization operates.[161] Culture can be a palace or a prison as it can invite opportunities or limit life to merely rely on what's already embedded.[162] Organizations structured from disparate groups, if coached to appreciate diverse instrumental values, bolster success opportunities through the expansion of terminal values by capitalizing on diverse attributes. A good example for excelling in diverse landscapes through multiplying values is exemplified in the United States of America (USA). It could be argued that diverse cultures and ethnicities are what made the USA a prosperous and coveted country. Conversely, this conglomeration of ethical groups and cultures could just as easily be undesirable for certain groups, if they are not valued.

> *In* Lassen, *we recognize and appreciate the differences, whether racial, social, gender, ethnical, or religious, in fellow crew members, and we intentionally avail the necessary tools, not to merely compensate for, but zero out these differences through objective-based practices and measures which allow everyone to achieve professional harmony and enjoy unbounded opportunities for personal and professional growth. This vision, in its purest form, transcends policy and directs changes in the hearts and minds!*
>
> —CDR Anthony Simmons,
> Commanding Officer

Leadership ethics

Ethics have an individual focus on what is right and wrong, which therein lies behavioral ethics and the dilemma of the "want self" and "should self."[163] Ethic, derived from the Greek word *ethos* (customs, conduct, or character), is the kind of values and morals an individual or a society deems desirable or appropriate.[164] Behavioral ethics and social beliefs are doing what someone is comfortable with and feels fits his/her perception.[165] Ethics also involve examining questions about right, wrong, good, evil, virtue, duty, obligation, rights, fairness, justice, and responsibility in human relationships with each other.[166] The challenge with ethics is found in the hypothesis that ethical decision-making is from a human perspective which oftentimes can be either egotistic or culturally biased.[167]

Are you as ethical as you think you are? It is human nature to act in the best interests of self as no element of scientific teaching and no facet of common interest can act to teach humans to share properties and privileges with equal consideration for all.[168] The ethical gap is the difference between one's behavior and one's perception of one's own behavior; a gap which traditional ethical approaches tend to ignore.[169] Garnering a common view on ethics within an organization can be tenuous when considering the disparities in individuals and societies across global landscapes. Attaining a common ethical view requires coaches to examine the second and third layer of culture implications. Leadership coaches must take calculated measures to bridge ethical gaps by refining ethical skills through hands-on experiences gained in cross-cultural training.

A relationship of mutual trust that transcends personal biases must be established to bridge ethical gaps. Along with being self-aware about how behavioral ethics shape organizations, coaches must also balance between morals and ethics and be adept at how culture and values impact ethical decisions if they are to promote environments conducive to universal growth. Once coaches have embraced and internalized the issues impacting the "want self," they can navigate blind spots. Individualistic thinking is replaced with communal approaches to realize a good ethical life where people relate to one another from a mutual vantage point.

Navigating blind spots through EI and values, flattening social identities, hurdling generations, and behavioral ethics

Although people research the implications of EI, values, cultures, social identities, generational difference, and ethics, the limitations of human reasoning require additional measures to remove blind spots. Coaches must continue to strengthen EI, better understand culture, values, social, and generational implications, and improve ethical self-awareness if they are to do right by coachees and improve organizational performance. Coaches must self-assess by looking inside to shed light on what they see on the outside; they must be committed to self-improvement. To lead change, coaches must be willing to reflect change within themselves. As Mahatma Gandhi once said, "Leaders need to be the change they want to see."

Learned behaviors that cause blind spots are usually associated with cultural makeups developed from culture types and dimensions. Human reasoning and ethical decisions are fraught with egotism and cultural biases accentuated by individual value systems. How do you close the gap between what you want to do and what you ought to do? To navigate blind spots, leadership coaches must transform individual values and beliefs into common views among disparate groups. This removes personal biases and accommodates the greater whole.

Ancient Indians surmised there are two types of knowledge: self-knowledge and knowledge of those around self. Cultivating the knowledge of self provides the footing for obtaining knowledge of those around you. A person can't gain knowledge of the environment around him/her until he/she understands the person within.[170] Mastering self-knowledge serves to translate what's inside to relate to the dynamics of diverse landscapes. This aligns cultural values and generational differences and flattens social identifies as it brings one in touch with his/her internal thinking. These phenomena influence self-reasoning, whereas the behavior supports self-images that could otherwise morph in rationalizing unethical behavior by changing one's definition of ethical behavior.[171]

EI and values alignment uprights leadership

Organizational structure and leadership approach must be flexible to allow best practices to enable shared values for growth and development among all entities. This structure is created through EI and values alignment. This alignment consists of coaches possessing the instrumental values to support the development of the five components of EI. One of the first priorities for global organizations is to align and balance individual values so they work in unison for the whole of the organization, independent of cultures. Because of the fundamental differences in individual personalities, performing MBTI profiles on key leaders is deemed appropriate.[172] Aligning and balancing key attributes of key stakeholders allow organizations to leverage diversity as a core competency to address varying situations to meet goals that may not align to singular individual values. Also, these assessments help to identify coaches' shortcomings.

Leadership turns upside down because leaders fail to recognize with whom they are interacting and are unable to appreciate the positions of those they lead. Coaches must recognize their own shortcomings to champion the development of others. It's more important for coaches to identify and address their own weaknesses than to highlight their strengths when serving others. Coaches must continue to bolster EI and improve values through self-reflection and self-analysis to work on strengths and weaknesses.[173] Professional endeavors are predicated on personal competence; employees cannot leave their nonprofessional self at home.[174] Personal and professional development act interdependently to manifest self-efficacy, whereas an individual strives to attain confidence in his/her ability to excel in human endeavors.[175] Essentially, one's professional life is predicated on personal development.

When leading diverse organizations, values provide the underpinning while EI facilitates the leadership skills and approaches; EI predicts behavior and attitudes in education.[176] EI components are dependent on values, whether intrinsic or acquired. The final dependency is terminal values (end state) that are dependent on instrumental values. Because of their elevated level of EI, transformational leaders can capitalize on diversity. They use diversity to expand opportunities as opposed to allowing it to constrain processes. The combination of values and EI yields self-assured leadership coaches with an appetite for serving others.

Flattening social identifies (culture)

Confident leaders don't have favorites.
—Anthony Simmons

Flattening social identities yields culture homogeneity. Executive coaches, regardless of beliefs, group affiliation, religions, and so forth, must establish common grounds through embracing a culture that represent everyone. When will in-groups and out-groups occupy the same room and space? Is navigating blind spots the panacea? In-group favoritism is a situation where people are intuitively more comfortable doing favors for people who look like themselves. People tend to be biased toward those for which they share an alma mater, religion, race, or gender.[177] How often do you hear the cliché "ducks pick ducks"? The reality is people are inclined to select those with whom they are most comfortable. People prefer to stay inside their comfort zone.

I vividly recall asking a fellow officer, who held an executive position on a prominent Navy staff, why the staff didn't feature more diverse officers. He replied that the admiral surrounded himself with those with whom he felt comfortable. I found this shortsighted, troubling, and linked to in-group favoritism. Regardless of background differences, leaders are responsible for the growth and development of everyone in their organization. They must embody the capacity to transcend in-group favoritism, which can be ameliorated through EI to subjugate blind spots.[178]

Occupying the same room requires integrating these two groups. Integration entails normalizing perspectives about social systems or, better yet, suppressing the behavior that creates divisiveness. The first step is recognizing that social identities must be overcome while the second step is overcoming learning anxiety. The best approach when pursuing change is strategically positioning wise change agents throughout the organization as these adept leaders transform the quality of relationships by collectively acting toward one purpose.[179] This facilitates a collectivist environment that places premium value on group membership and health rather than personal ambitions. This collective approach stems from the forming of autotelic relationships that help entities see matters as symbiotic, hence finding inherent value in whatever they are doing.[180] These relationships encourage leadership wisdom which mitigates learning anxieties and egoism, whereas the organization takes precedence over individuals.

Leadership coaches have an ethical obligation to create and maintain a culture that encourages perpetual development for everyone despite their innate leadership skills. Navigating blind spots helps to see the difference between how you think you act on cultures and what the client sees from his vantage point.[181] Relationships require constant interactions on a mutual playing field with a stabilizing agent. The clan culture, which encourages universal development, facilitates this stabilizing agent as it portends utilitarianism and fosters relationships while the collectivism dimension reinforces the conditions by ensuring the glass remains full. This cultural element provides the magnetism for a point of confluence for mutual ethical decisions.

The flattening of social identities allows coaches a common perspective on disparate cultures to develop global leaders independent of origin. To satisfy this leadership charge, leaders must possess the capacity to appreciate everyone's respective social identity and collectively develop all cultures. However, the challenge is subrogating in-group favoritism to communal opportunities.

> *All I'm saying is simply this: that all mankind is tied together, all life is interrelated, and we are all caught in an inescapable network of mutuality, tied in a single garment of identity. Whatever affects one directly, affects all indirectly. For some strange reason, I can never be what I ought to be until you are what you ought to be. And you can never be what I ought to be until I am what I ought to be. This is the interrelated structure of reality.*
> —Dr. Martin Luther King Jr., Oberlin College Commencement, 1965

Leadership development efforts must take into the account the personal, social, and professional identities of corporate leaders holistically as they include integrated and mutually inclusive attributes.[182] These efforts must involve personal expansion or development centered around the attaining of knowledge, experiencing change, advance, or progress to experience better efficiency in leadership responsibilities, procedures, and human development.[183] Integrated attributes personify a collaborative mindset to realize social awareness and social facility.[184] These social attributes flatten social identities to facilitate coaching in diverse cultures. Social identities are also critical in a collective sense because followers use stereotypes, based on social relationships, to judge how they feel about their leaders' performance.[185]

The US Navy training, despite working in host nations' backyards, must make conscientious efforts to avoid episodes of imposing US culture norms on international communities. Conversely, the best training US Navy leaders can receive is on ways to identify and remove their blind spots as these methods prevent leaders from knowing what they don't know.[186] A good example of overcoming blind spots is communicated by Gen. Jim Mattis when he posited that nations must understand that having the preponderance of forces doesn't equate to imposing their culture on other nations.[187] Instead, trust is the glue that permits coalition militaries to work harmoniously together as strength comes from an uncompromising spirit of collaboration.[188] Also, military cultural training must continue to evolve into understanding the underlying theories behind multicultural behavior rather than making assumptions based on observed surface behaviors and artifacts.

Hurdling the generational wall

If generational differences are not part of the strategic structural organizational calculus, blind spots can develop across generations. During residency at Regent University, I overheard a student suggest separating legacy employees from new generation workers as the best approach to manage amid five generations. The suggestion was made because this person felt separation curtails the bickering and mitigates inherent differences in views. I was flabbergasted by this assertion. I interjected by suggesting that by not integrating the disparate cultures, they were missing opportunities to capitalize on the values each generation offers. Moreover, separation would cause the organization to miss the chance to develop dyadic relationships across generations. These dyadic relationships would benefit the organization because they would foster an atmosphere where team members would rely one another for personal and professional growth and organizational success.[189] I suggested that each generation has immense attributes to offer one another while working alongside each other. Generations must be integrated throughout organizations to transform differences to common strengths and preclude generational blind spots.

Behavioral ethics (ethical self-awareness)

> *Bounded ethicality places limits on ethics*
> *which generate blind spots.*
> —Anthony Simmons

People don't realize that their ethical judgments have inherent biases. These biases cause them to behave in ways that they would condemn if they had keener self-awareness.[190] Two forms of behavioral or normative ethics about making decisions about what is right resonate in decisionist and virtue ethics. Decisionist ethics are what one ought to do when faced with two courses of action. Virtue ethics are just doing what is right.[191] Decisionist ethics resonate in in-group and out-group leadership matters, which will be expounded on in chapter 8. Behavioral ethics help mitigate this behavior through the utility of two cognitive systems, which are referred to as system 1 and system 2 thinking.[192] System 1 is our intuitive way of processing information in an implicit, effortless, and emotional manner. System 2 is the more effortful, explicit, and logical approach to decision-making.[193] System 2 requires applying the lens of behavioral ethics that allows one, regardless of group affiliation, to see the ethical implications of decisions more clearly and make choices that better aligns with values.[194] It is incumbent on leaders to adhere to their embedded values system and keep it transparent with employees while being sensitive to morality and ethics as they relate to attitude and behavior.[195]

Virtue ethics suppress ethical egoism and the erratic behavior of human reasoning.[196] Ethical egoism enables blind spots to occur because it considers actions beneficial to an individual based on self-interest; the good consequences for the individual outweigh the consequences placed upon others.[197] One can overcome cognitive limitations by doing what is morally right. Ethical decisions hinge on virtue ethics, deontology, and utilitarianism.[198] Coaches must not pursue relevance; they must see their duties as a vocation free of temptations and egotism.[199] Leadership coaches apply the following measures to develop communal relationships that suppress blind spots:[200]

- **Virtue Ethics:** Human perspective of what kind of person one ought to be to model the good life—for example, moral excellence.
- **Deontology:** The focus on the nature of the action or what underscores the ethical behavior. Does the action or ethical behavior adhere to moral principles?
- **Utilitarianism:** The consequences of the action with focus on the idea of the greater good for the most people. The conduct is ethical if it does better for a greater number of people than it harms.

Successful global leaders must exude wisdom, dedication, a tireless work ethic, and be enterprising and authentic because cross-cultural leadership requires one to not only identify with his/her shortcomings but also have the psychological capital to discard some learned behaviors and pursue requisite intellectual and social capital.[201] Transformational leaders with the capacity to communicate an authentic vision (terminal value) that creates an autotelic culture will be successful global leaders.

While commanding the destroyer USS *Lassen*, I once addressed the crew by stating: "Although we come from different parts of the country and different ethnicities, we all joined the Navy with a common vision to grow as individuals while serving our country to ensure national security." The quote facilitated alignment and authenticity.

In summary, this chapter demonstrates that navigating blind spots allows leadership coaches to overcome individual perspectives on cultures, values, social institutions, generations, and ethics to acquire a renewed view on personal and professional attributes. It highlights how coaching is essential to getting leadership right side up in times of eroding interpersonal skills and value-based leadership due to AI and bounded ethics. It emphasizes the benefit of doing what is right and how to integrate in-groups and out-groups into the same room under one belief and value system.

Coaches must be competent and self-assured to act based not only on what they ought to do but also what motivates them to do it.[202] This behavior personifies the ontology of ethical leadership.[203] Navigating blind spots leverages EI components and assessments to equip leadership coaches with requisite skills to address personal shortcomings that stem from culture beliefs, values, ethics, and generational differences. It bridges ethical gaps, leverages values, and flattens social identities to normalize global landscapes. Navigating blind spots judges the distance (varies with respect to social identities) between the coach and coachee to determine the halfway point. The renewed vision that results from this conciliation helps the coach and coachee establish common perspectives to facilitate a healthy coaching conversation and pathway to success.

CHAPTER 5

Coaching Conversation Builds Trust and Engenders Symmetrical Growth

Coaching conversation yields symmetrical growth

Coaches must be coached to enhance their EI prowess.
—Anthony Simmons

Coaching portends a coach catapulting a coachee to the next level of success by meeting him/her halfway. The ability to meet requires the coach to identify his/her own location and to possess the wherewithal to judge the distance between themselves and the coachee to meet the coachee halfway. Halfway is considered the point of mutual perspectives based on social status, generations, and culture norms.

Once the halfway point is identified, the coach and the coachee can move symmetrically through the coaching conversation to achieve mutual success for the coach, coachee, and organization. Accordingly, chapters 3 and 4 provided the enabling principles that allow the coach and coachee to colocate and interact using a common lens. This synergistic interaction characterizes a coaching conversation that consists of an intricate and trusting relationship that draws out the coachee's introspection while allowing the coach to grow as well. Through the application of EI components, self-assessments, and navigating blind spots, the coaching conversation marks the culmination point for realizing the foundational (means) element for OW. It represents the coach-coachee melding pot. This melding pot hinges on the four parts of a coaching conversation that are shaped by the ICF core competencies (https://coachfederation.org/core-competencies).[204] While chapters 3 and 4 addressed how to establish common grounds, this chapter illustrates how to choreograph the symmetrical walk to OW while scaling cultures through empowerment.

This symmetrical walk begins by leveraging the coaching conversation to merge the leader and aspiring leader's perspectives and drawing out the aspiring leader's introspection to design a call to action to cultivate the path to success. This chapter describes how the four parts of the coaching conversation are used to facilitate the relationship between the coach and coachee. Then it leverages the ICF core competencies as a framework to illustrate how the coaching conversation cultivates a path for the coach and coachee to best position themselves and the organization for optimal performance. The process involves moving the coach and coachee through the filters in *coaching triangulation*. The framework also manifests a leadership succession for the coach. These core competencies were described in chapter 2. Therefore, I will only summarize how they will influence the interaction between the coach and coachee. It is helpful to note that the coaching conversation is distinguished by the *nature* of the interaction between the coach and coachee.

Reflecting a dialogue of relative coequals, the interaction personifies a symbiotic relationship between the leadership coach and coachee where each is helped to grow. Again, coaches must be coached for continuous personal development and professional growth. This approach to leadership development is appropriate in global landscapes because diverse and dynamic conditions demand an influential leadership methodology between the two coequals compared to the traditional leader-follower relationship. This influential approach entails engaging in a bidirectional conversation that engenders cooperative problem solving.

The collaborative approach to problem solving is magnified by the enduring and dyadic relationship of coequals mutually championing the progress of one another. This is key because, like trust, there is a common misconception that the coaching relationship is directional with the expectation that the person in the higher position is the only person who needs to exude trust. Dyadic relationships must be underscored by mutual trust between the parties; trust is a bi-direction tenet.

Mutual trust is quintessential to the coaching conversation as it allows the coach and coachee to share perspectives to make one another their best selves. The learning is symbiotic as coaches are coached through the feedback gleaned from asking powerful questions and performing intuitive listening. The coaching conversation is edified through the ICF core competencies.

The ICF core competencies, established standards, are most appropriate to scope and drive the coaching conversation. The core competencies refer to coaching as partnering with coachees in a thought-provoking and creative form that inspires the coachees to maximize their personal and professional attributes. In parallel with its viewpoint on coaching, ICF core competencies suggest coaching is a teaching method for fostering mature relationships, healthier thinking, and optimal decision-making amid disparate groups for those in leadership roles (http://www.wisegeek.net/what-is-leadership-coaching.htm).

However, coaching is a client-based relationship involving the following steps: (1) coach and coachee gain insight from the coach by asking powerful (open-ended) questions, (2) the coach listens intuitively while the coachee reveals his/her introspection, (3) coach and coachee design a call to action, and (4) the coach supports the coachee's actions and ensures they are properly executed.[205] The coaching conversation personifies an encouraging coaching intervention for optimal performance and continued success. The open and honest coachee-based structure of the interaction is the fulcrum to cocreating and effectively communicating. It is ideal for solving complex problems amid uncertainty and fostering ongoing change in diverse global landscapes.

Shaping the coaching conversations with ICF core competencies

Coaching consists of developing aspiring leaders through listening, asking questions, designing action, and supporting the transformation through *servantship*. The coaching conversation accentuates this process through a more intuitive approach to listening to draw out the coachee's introspective through open-ended questions. The coaching conversation is illuminated by facilitating a call to action and supporting learning and results through influential measures while suspending judgment.[206] The intuitive approach to listening explores the underlying factors to draw out the meaning from the story to deepen the learning.[207] This intuitive listening and discovery serve the coach as a teaching tool as well as engenders growth for both the coach and coachee to enhance organizational performance.

The coaching concept is the bridge for connecting these tools to realize continued success for leaders, aspiring leaders, and organizations across myriad sectors. The transformational and enduring aspect of coaching is rooted in the coaching conversation as it connects people to performance through a tangible communication process.[208] Coaching mimics authentic leadership by providing a sense of mission, inspiration, emotional support, and intellectual stimulation.[209] Furthermore, coaching is about the relationship between the coach and coachee where, as illustrated in ICF core competencies, trust and intimacy must be established while a genuine concern for the coachee's professional development and personal welfare must be observed.

Setting the foundation

Before a coaching conversation transpires, a coaching foundation must be established to set the guidelines and standards to gain a clear understanding of responsibilities and expectations between the leadership coach and coachee. This foundation comprises meeting the ethical guidelines and professional standards and establishing the coaching agreement as described in chapter 2. The foundation is ascertained by the results of the self-assessments that help to determine if the coach and coachee can identify a halfway point. Moreso, the process pivots on an initial assessment to best shape the coaching conversation—it sets the stage and demonstrates care.

Co-creating the relationship

The assessments described in chapter 3 provide a platform of open dialogue to build a collaborative, dyadic relationship. This platform serves as the underpinning for the coach-coachee relationship as the success of one enable the success of the other.[210] Dyadic personalities develop when one needs another person continually to know who he really is.[211] All else pales regarding relationships because the goal is to build trust, respect, integrity, and honesty, which are the fruits of strong and genuine relationships.[212] Once the foundation is established, a coaching relationship is cocreated to develop trust and foster a transparent and unbiased dialogue to unearth underlying assumptions to navigate blind spots. As discussed in chapter 2, this process involves establishing trust and intimacy with the coachee and displaying a coaching presence. Assessments are also pivotal to properly influencing and cocreating this dialogue as they provide the basis for relating to the coachees' concerns and feeling their pulse. Establishing trust is value-based. One of the most instrumental values is honesty as is it stands alone in fostering trust and building relationships. Once trust is established, the leader demonstrates to the aspiring leader she/he cares through sharing unfavorable but similar experiences to establish common grounds.[213] These common grounds enable an environment of trust for transparent and authentic relationships to evolve.[214]

Everyone has something in common. The challenge is identifying it. The coaching conversation helps locate these common threads. For example, when meeting with the media upon arriving in Maizuru, Japan, I shared a story with local media about how I could relate to their small-town culture as it mirrored my upbringing and hometown culture. I communicated how much it meant to me to have hailed from a working-class culture underpinned by hard work and humble beginnings. This story afforded me instant credibility and established trust between my organization and the citizens of the town. The exchange was highlighted in the local newspaper the following day.

Communicating effectively

Effective communications are the nucleus of the coaching relationship and building trust and intimacy that afford a platform conducive to drawing out strengths and weaknesses of the coachee.[215] This platform consists of active listening (intuitive listening), asking powerful questioning, and direct communication. The open discussion must be underscored by "unconditional positive regard" to establish a platform of trust and intimacy that enable open and unguarded relationshipshttps://christiancoaches.com/wp-content/uploads/2017/10/Competencies-Edited-Final-2017.pdf).

Active listening. Coaching affords a forum for listening to what's inside the coachee through active listening. Active listening enables the process and encourages an environment conducive to unadulterated feedback. This feedback and information exchange go beyond surface talk and delves into feeling one another's pulse to assist in determining the appropriate path forward. As discussed in chapter 4, the conversation starts from a mutual location to cultivate the optimal path for success.

This cultivation process hinges on the coach making the coachee feel safe and secure by displaying inviting listening signs, such as leaning in, head nodding, and eagerness to empathize.[216] Although comparable stories can sometimes be misconstrued as signs of not listening closely, in this regard, sharing personal stories is one of the best measures for creating common threads.[217]

Powerful questions. Powerful questions enable an aspiring leader to draw together the threads for him/herself in the most appropriate way.[218] Coaching assists leaders in developing skills or reinvigorating dormant skills by allowing them to surface their introspective through asking powerful questions and listening closely as they reflect. Coaching is a non-authoritative relationship that focuses on the coachee and allows him/her to associate with previously unrecognized talents she/he possesses.[219]

This stage of the conversation offers questions to help the coachee align what they think they know to what they ought/need to know. The self-efficacy that evolves from the interaction instills beliefs in individuals so that the difficult tasks they once avoided are viewed as welcomed opportunities.[220] The questions are open-ended to evoke discovery, insight, and buy-in from the coachee as it is the self-revelation of his/her introspection that drives this insight and discovery.

Direct communication. Providing feedback to the open-ended questions while suspending judgment exemplify direct communication. The objective is to draw out the best in the coachee. It entails getting to the root of matters to ensure goals and objectives are aligned for the coaching session. The coach must ensure the coachee's perspective is in alignment or agreeable with the agenda communicated. Coaching is a partnership, and it requires quality feedback and information exchange between the coach and coachee. This partnership is what separates coaching from mentoring and counseling as the information sharing between the coach and coachee is unmatched.

Also, in the existential approach, the coach and coachee development does not require a transition. Instead, it involves the coach asking the coachee questions about his/her worldview to help substantiate the coachee's inter-relationally attuned awareness and understanding to champion his/her own cause.[221] These coaching skills are enhanced through insight gleaned from coachee's creative thinking. Asking deep questions of the coachee creates a bond of honor and value between the coach and coachee because asking critical questions indicates a deep level of care.[222]

Facilitating learning and results to support the symmetrical walk

Facilitated learning is the nucleus of the coach-coachee interaction. The core of the conversation is predicated on implementing methodologies to facilitate learning, and the associated results are used to design the best call to action for the coachee based on his/her introspective. The facilitating and learning process is comprised of creating awareness, designing actions, planning and goal setting, and managing progress and accountability. This stage of the process is transformational in that it involves elevating the level of motivation and morality in both the coach and coachee.[223] Facilitating and learning, like transformational coaching, is the art of assisting people to enhance their effectiveness in a way they feel helped.[224] I find a parallel between helping someone and the origin of coaching which was derived in the stagecoach days as getting someone from point A to point B.[225] Coaching is facilitating the requisite actions, plans, goals, and measures to take the coachee from where she/he is to where he or she wants to go through personal transformation—this takes place through relational behavior, intuitive listening, influence, responsibility, accountability, and empowerment.[226]

Creating awareness. While peer coaching involves a relationship between a highly experienced and lesser experienced individual, it is not a one-size-fits-all approach—each situation is unique and demands the appropriate framework.[227] This conviction is underscored by my experience with coaching as a commanding officer on a destroyer, leading amid multiple generations. As their coach, my job entailed making a personal transformation in my approach to get officers and sailors from where they thought they were to where they needed to be as professional mariners and tacticians. Once awareness was created, I would assist the officers and sailors in designing actions with the help of assigned coaches.

Designing actions. When designing action, it is incumbent on the coach to relate to the coachee by developing an autotelic relationship to sense the value the action provided for the coachee. Coaches encourage the action and support the process while being careful not to design or dictate the coachee's course as coaching facilitates. Coaching is a closed-loop system that helps the leader and aspiring leader determine one another's vantage to mutually devise the required course to accommodate the needs of both. This relationship, fundamental to leadership, is about the coach displaying empathy toward the coachee to best determine how to cultivate his/her success.[228] The coaching conversation not only affords a vehicle for which to judge the relative position between the coach and coachee, but it also allows the coach and coachee to achieve synergy and grow symmetrically through an integrated plan of action.

Planning and goal setting. Coaching provides an atmosphere that is conducive to growth, gaining confidence, and overcoming fears as opposed to lifting someone from negative situations through authoritative measures.[229] Coaching facilitates learning and results as it doesn't involve having all the answers. Coaches ask powerful question to improve their situational awareness during the exploration and discovery process. This process bolsters the self-awareness of the coachee so she/he can devise a list of self-generated options on which to base goals.[230]

Managing progress and accountability. This step is dependent on the substance extracted from the coaching conversation where intuitive listening enables the coachee to gain perspective and assess the pertinent position from which to design the path forward. The follow-on actions determined in the coaching conversation comprise considering culture differences and life position to guide the course to arrive at the desired location. This action requires developing a call to action and supporting the process to realize the vision.[231] A strategic narrative is required to govern the process. The four pillars of OW are responsibility, accountability, loyal, and trust (I will expand on this in chapter 8). In this regard, accountability and trust are bidirectional and keep both the coach and coachee honest in executing the call to action and ascertaining the agreed-upon support is in place to help the coachee realize the defined vision.

A call to action commands transparency and authentic leadership. Authentic leadership mimics coaching in a manner that affects the coach and the coachee during interactions whereas coaches must develop the coachee through an active process as opposed to the passive behavior resident in transactional leadership. Rewarding people for their efforts is passive while transforming them by providing a sense of mission, inspiration, emotional support, and intellectual stimulation is active behavior.[232] Transformational leadership is sustaining because it connects people to performance through a real-time communication process.[233] This process serves to further sharpen the EI components for both the leader and aspiring leader as they mutually oversee progress.

This is the step in the process where social skills are pivotal to moving people in a direction of greater promise.[234] These social skills must address the same strategies required to navigate blind spots discussed in chapter 4. I always find it fitting to share my experience when leading across generations during my tenure as commanding officer in USS *Lassen*. Considering the generational gap as an executive coach, the onus was on me to identify and implement measures that allowed me to relate to new-generation officers. The measures mimicked me (as the coach) growing in lockstep with the coachees to relate and identify the best position to support their learning process. I would submit that it was my ability to understand the importance of relating to officers across myriad generations that enabled my efficacy as a commander during my time in USS *Lassen*.

Although I didn't have the formal training on applying assessments at the time, upon observing an officer struggle to earn his deck-officer qualification after three failed oral boards, I personally administered an assessment of his critical-thinking skills and realized he was struggling with cognitive dissonance. It was a noticeable disconnect between the expectations of the qualification process against the officer's perspective on the oral board performance. First, I had to share stories about my professional shortcomings to develop a relationship.[235] As a measure to empower the officer, the need to develop a qualification process through him became apparent. Essentially, I enabled the officer the act through empowering the design and manage progress.[236] The officer was encouraged to read an article on critical thinking to gain a better understanding of his roadblocks. As a result of reading the article, the officer was able to better self-assess to cultivate a viable path forward.

Coaching conversation flattens social identity to facilitate global leadership development

The vignette provides an example of a US Navy (USN) and South Korea Navy (ROKN) coaching platform to illustrate how coaching in global environments facilitates leadership development amid disparate cultures. The coaching nation and coached nation represent the coach and coachee, respectively.[237]

This book leverages the ICF core competencies to frame measures a global leaders can use to optimize leadership development amid disparate cultures (https://coachfederation.org/core-competencies). The author uses firsthand experience from engagements between the USN and ROKN to demonstrate how flat social identities are manifested and support leadership development during global military operations. Effectively, a coaching foundation is established to develop trust and foster open and unbiased dialogue between leaders and partnership nations. Once the foundation is in place, a relationship is cocreated to best unearth underlying assumptions. The cocreated relationship then evolves into a platform of effective communications conducive to drawing out strengths of the partnering nation's culture. Finally, the conversation culminates in the implementation of methodologies to facilitate cultural learning and the associated results used to design the best leadership development approach for respective cultures. Overall, the flat social identity, which is developed from an intricate conversation between global leaders and partnering nations, fosters an environment of effective leadership development by removing cultural barriers.

In *Handbook for Leadership Development*, Van Veslor et al. claim social identity influences one's perception and behavior based on power dynamics associated with resources, status, and privilege.[238] The authors feel this situation morphs into dominate and nondominated groups that can create barriers for the development of leaders. However, leadership coaching, a proven process for developing leaders, provides a viable platform for suppressing these barriers. In *Christian Coaching*, Collins deems coaching as assisting others to get them from where they are to where they desire to be.[239] In the context of cultures, coaching helps countries to achieve flat social identities by facilitating the means to draw out embedded resources and carefully considering environmental factors that best support appropriate leadership development opportunities. Flat social identities represent a social construct where resources, status, and privilege do not dictate the leadership development approaches because they are normalized through a coaching conversation.

To expound further, coaches, unlike leaders and mentors, do not impose their expert views on coachees to determine the coachees' path for success. Rather, coaching, as illustrated by Stoltzfus in *Leadership Coaching*, facilitates a conversation of intuitive listening and open-ended questions that stir the coachee toward hidden attributes and then assists in constructing a plan to retrieve them by supporting the coachee until the attributes are fused into his/her leadership fabric.[240] Coaching global nations is parallel to coaching individuals but expands the process into assessing cultural locations to best determine the appropriate methodology for uniform social identity to support leadership development from the vantage point of the partnering country. Examining coaching is best scoped through the ICF core competencies of setting the foundation, cocreating relationships, communicating effectively, facilitating learning, and measuring results to determine the best method to optimize leadership development for disparate countries. As Hunt and Weintraub suggest in *The Coaching Organization*, coaching benefits the coach, coachee, and the organization. In that vein, this model benefits USN, ROKN, and the country of South Korea.[241] The USN aim was to coach ROKN to take the lead on regional national security efforts.

Establishing the foundation

Setting the foundation consists of meeting ethical guidelines and professional standards while establishing the coaching agreement. It was incumbent on the USN to ensure the ROKN clearly understood the covenant of the relationship and could discern between coaching and mentoring. The guidelines for the engagement were delineated in a memorandum of agreement (MOA), which made it clear the ROKN would be afforded a safe learning environment. Just as in a coaching agreement, all expectations and recourses were made evident at the outset of each training event. Along with clearly laying out the expectations for each Navy, the MOA addressed cultural norms, beliefs, and traditions of South Korea.

Establishing the foundation consisted of the USN training its leaders on the difference between cultures and values. For example, in *Balancing Individual and Organizational Values*, Hultman and Gellerman assert values are something people embody, and cultures reside in countries are made up of people of a multitude of values. They conclude organizations (countries in this case) do not have values. Rather, countries consist of cultures that are grounded on the collective values of the individuals that live in that country.[242] Training on cultures proved critical because it allowed the USN to cocreate the relationship with the ROKN.

Cocreating the relationship

Cocreating the relationship provides the underpinning for a flat social identity, owing to the collaborative environment of trust, mutual respect, and openness. The objective is to establish a presence that powers the strength of the partnering country to facilitate trust, a sum-of-the-whole approach, to leadership development while suppressing proclivities of dominant cultures to resort to the sum-of-the-parts stance. However, for the relationship to manifest and baseline expectations, a culture assessment is performed by the coaching nation to glean understanding and gain appreciation for the partnering nation's cultural and environmental attributes. This baseline helps the coaching nation establish a genuine coaching presence and continue to curtail tendencies to default to dominate social identities. In

Psychometrics in Coaching, Passmore credited assessments as the key to establishing a baseline with a client to determine the level and approach for engagement.[243]

After the baseline was established, and the USN gained an appreciation of the ROKN attributes and had unmasked blind spots, both navies then engaged in a coaching dialogue to cocreate insights and understanding. Together, both navies managed to shape meaning and develop new or alternatives for events, situations, and tasks to enhance leadership development opportunities through practical measures. These events allowed the ROKN to not only realize its attributes but to solidify the cocreated relationship and instill requisite confidence for conducting dynamic at-sea exercises/engagements. Essentially, once the underpinning was in place, the two navies were prepared to partake in at-sea training events while bolstering the coaching relationship through communicating with powerful questions, intuitive listening, and observing candid information exchange amid a flat social identity.

Communicating at the right level and in the right space

Communicating at the right level and in the right space is predicated on having the cultural wherewithal to know what questions to ask and the willingness to continue to sharpen the saw by listening intuitively to draw out the coachee key attributes. The conversation may require the coaching nation to share stories that relate to events the partnering nation has experienced so they will feel better sharing information and revealing weaknesses. The leadership coaches must possess the requisite self-awareness to know what open-ended questions are best suited for the coachees and apply intuitive listening to engender insights and enrich the conversation for optimal leadership development.

For the USN and ROKN coaching conversation, USN leaders empowered ROKN leaders by allowing them to occupy the seats during training events so they could gain confidence while driving the solution set on their own accord. Essentially, the USN observed what is referred to as reach-through training, which is akin to facilitating learning and results to allow the coachee to self-solve any potential problems. The reach-through training allowed the coaching nation to get below partnering countries' artifacts to better understand why they took certain actions. The coaching nation learned that most of the actions were culturally driven. This is why it is so important for the coaching nation to remain keenly aware of cultural norms and refrain from imposing dominant social identities.

Notwithstanding, to properly facilitate training, USN leaders had to continue to be intentional in reinforcing events from the perspective of the partnering nation. In accord with Van Veslor's et al. view on expert leaders, USN leadership coaches needed to sustain the capacity to help countries to be inclusive of all opportunities and use shared identities to sustain commitments and move in a coordinated fashion for facilitating learning and measuring results.

Facilitating learning and measuring results

Facilitating learning and measuring results comprise creating awareness, designing actions, planning and goal setting, and managing progress and accountability. USN and ROKN cross-pollinated leadership coaches into one another's ships for cultural ingratiation to create opportunities for continuous learning and accountability. The at-sea events were designed from analysis and insights from in-port events, stemming from powerful questions. These opportunities involved practical exercises that enabled the collection of relevant information to ascertain planned actions were being observed, evaluated, and tracked. For measuring results, feedback tools were at the disposal of USN leadership coaches and ROKN coachees to determine near real-time course corrections to stay on the planned course of movement. However, this called for unvarnished feedback.

Feedback was provided through direct communications to gauge success and design follow-on events to expand learning opportunities. Basically, learning was facilitated by placing ROKN entities in key roles (call to action) and supporting them in performing the call to action. Just as coaching is designed to help cultures with less resources determine ways to get more resources by facilitating the access to resources, at-sea events between the USN and ROKN were designed to flex partnering nation's resources through situational facilitation. This facilitation was scaled on situational requirements. The USN adopted the situational leadership model provided in Figure 5, presented by Northouse in *Leadership Coaching*, as a mean to coach based on the level of proficiency regarding feedback from each respective coaching event.[244] The overarching goal was to coach the ROKN to reach S4 level where the USN could delegate responsibilities to the ROKN once they demonstrated the capacity to execute the regional commander's role.

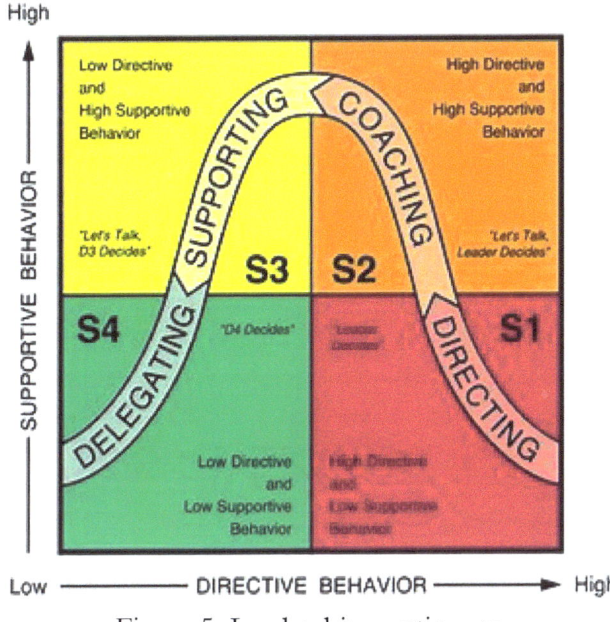

Figure 5. Leadership continuum

Conclusion

A flat social identity affords a formidable platform for global leadership development amid disparate cultures because it increases global reach. The flat design is manifested through a coaching construct that yields transparency in assessing cultures to establish a baseline for proper development. Leadership coaches must know the coachee's location to determine where she/he desires to go and the level of influence needed to get her/him there. Coaching facilitates a cocreated relationship for mutually (removes biases) assessing cultures from the vantage of everyone involved while suppressing would-be dominate proclivities. Flattened social identities are a leadership imperative in today's interconnected and virtual landscape as cultures must be as common as the networks that enable shared global communications. Everyone must be in sync and on the same social accord.

Leadership coaches must value the assets each group brings to the table whether they are in-group or out-group. Perhaps, the new and operative term *inter-group* affords the best solution for sustained, optimal leadership development. Leadership coaching is the mechanism to flatten social identities and transform diversity of thought into strengths. Van Veslor et al. suggest leadership coaching is an ongoing process. Therefore, coaches must continue to coach and be coached by partnering countries to collectively flatten social identities as flat social identities are viable platforms for global leadership development.

In summary, this chapter illustrated how a coaching conversation framed by the ICF core competencies provides the ingredient to conduct a conversation to move the coachee through cultural differences by using a coaching intervention. It prepares the coach and coachee for mutual growth through a symmetrical walk to achieve optimal performance for the coach, coachee, and organization holistically.

PART 3 (WAYS)

RELOCATING TO GAIN OPTIMAL POSITIONING: COACH AND COACHEE SYMMETRICAL ASCENSION THROUGH CULTURE AGNOSTICISM AND EMPOWERMENT THROUGH A COACHING ORGANIZATION

Coaching a culture of empowerment through servantship!

CHAPTER 6
Culture Agnosticism through Homogeneous Perspectives

The research for this chapter is based on both academia and my firsthand experience leading amid disparate cultures while performing engagements in sixty-three countries over a span of twenty-eight years. The visits involved partaking in social intelligence endeavors by getting in the trenches with host nations to explore cultural norms, beliefs, and values through partaking in goodwill, community relations, culture excursions, recreational events, and so on. On many occasions, the visits consisted of meeting with and conducting personal calls on executive leaders and dignitaries, such as governors, mayors, commerce officials, ambassadors, and senior military officials. Having the opportunity to ingratiate myself into these cultures afforded invaluable opportunities to obtain cultural competence. I also gained a level of cultural agility to the point where my culture no longer dominated my perspective. This allowed me to suspend my opinions to become *culturally agnostic*, which means transcending culture by developing metacultural behaviors to be effective across cultures.[245] These acquired skills underscored my capacity to foster environments of cultural homogeneity for leading in global landscapes.

In chapter 4, I discussed navigating blind spots and the causal actors from which they are generated to enable a renewed vision for nurturing good ethical decisions to quell any propensity for ethnocentric behavior and in-group favoritism. Chapter 4 also explained how bridging cultural gaps eradicates cultural biases and sets the stage for culture agnosticism. This chapter illustrates how leaders and aspiring leaders can achieve optimal performance through a homogeneous view on culture through being agnostic. This view requires being impartial about personal beliefs, values, and social identities. The chapter also discusses how cultural competence expands perspectives and aligns leaders and aspiring leaders independent of their countries and societies of origin. Next, it applies firsthand experiences getting in the trenches with allied navies to ingratiate myself into their cultures, learning to appreciate of their perspectives by exploring espoused values and underlying assumptions. Then the thesis explains how cultural agility manifests cultural competency and generates a firsthand appreciation of how disparate groups value their respective cultures. The chapter culminates by telling how the integration of culture competence, ingratiation, and agility yield cultural agnosticism for global leaders. Hence, the confluence of cultural competence and ingratiation engenders culture agility, whereas the end state yields cultural agnosticism. Cultural agnosticism is the linchpin to leading amid disparate cultures in global landscapes. Homogenous cultures are agnostic and must be manifested when leading in global expanses. Furthermore, becoming culturally agnostic requires culture exposure and openness to change that also resonates with navigating blind spots.

I would argue the first step to becoming culturally agnostic is possessing self-awareness, self-regulation, and empathy to connect to disparate cultures. Basic beliefs developed from learned behaviors do not bode well amid disparate groups in cross-cultural landscapes. Global leadership is predicated on developing and sustaining trust through coaching aspiring leaders to understand cultural norms of respective countries. The developed understanding helps to ensure expectations are aligned to common purposes. This commonality personifies cultural homogeneity that is inevitably realized through a coaching conversation such as the USN-ROKN example presented in chapter 5.

> *When it comes to culture, there is only one goal: "Every Sailor and Marine—of all races, genders, religions, and ethnicities—must treat one another with dignity and respect." It is not just about doing the right thing. It is about ensuring our Navy and Marine Corps will be the most talented, most combat ready, and most committed force possible.*
> —Carlos Del Toro, US Navy Secretary, *Defense News*, September 2021

Differently from leadership in homogeneous environments, global leadership is more complex and requires examining cultures beyond the surface to unearth what drives cultural norms.[246] Global leaders are not born but made. They must acquire three key global leadership attributes. They must invest time and effort to develop the following competencies:

1) global mindset—cultural competence as an ability to develop palatable relationships across cultures
2) global entrepreneurship—cultural agility to engender the capacity to generate values across cultural boundaries
3) global citizenship—culturally ingratiation into disparate cultures to seek a positive contribution[247]

To further expound, a global mindset is a matter of looking beyond domestic or individual views associated with personal experiences and exploring other cultures to bolster cultural competency.[248] In turn, cultural competence is created through a global mindset that consists of looking beyond the artifacts and deceptive outer layer and exploring the espoused values to unearth underlying assumptions and cultural attitudes.[249] Cultural entrepreneurship is demonstrating the cultural agility to reach across cultural boundaries and create value through partnerships among disparate cultures.[250] And finally, culture ingratiation benefits everyone involved and garners buy-in across all entities.[251]

Figure 6a is a depiction of the three layers of cultural competencies in the arrangement of an onion. The observable outer surface indicates what is perceived, the middle consists of attitudes of unspoken opinion about conditions, and the inner most circle involves values based on embedded assumptions that are difficult to articulate even by those who are familiar with the culture.[252]

Figure 6a. Schein culture rings

To further illuminate the structure of cultures, Figure 6b provides[253]

- artifacts or the tangibles that can be seen and observed at the surface layer of a culture;
- espoused beliefs and values that determines one's opinion predicated on beliefs about how things should be rather than how they are; and
- basic underlying assumptions, unconsciously taken for granted values and beliefs, that are embedded assumptions that can't be articulated by those who are well-versed in the culture.

Culturally agile leaders must peel back the cultural rings in global landscapes to reduce the artifacts and observable surface to indicators that serve as entering arguments for evaluating espoused beliefs and cultural attitudes. This peeling back determines whether underlying assumptions and cultural values are conducive to success during VUCA conditions.[254] In this regard, there are five dimensions of personality variation that can be used to score cultures: openness to experience versus rigidity, conscientiousness versus undependability, extraversion versus introversion, agreeableness versus ill-temperedness, and neuroticism versus emotionally stability.[255] These dimensions are pivotal to uncovering cultural attitudes, cultural values, and underlying assumptions.

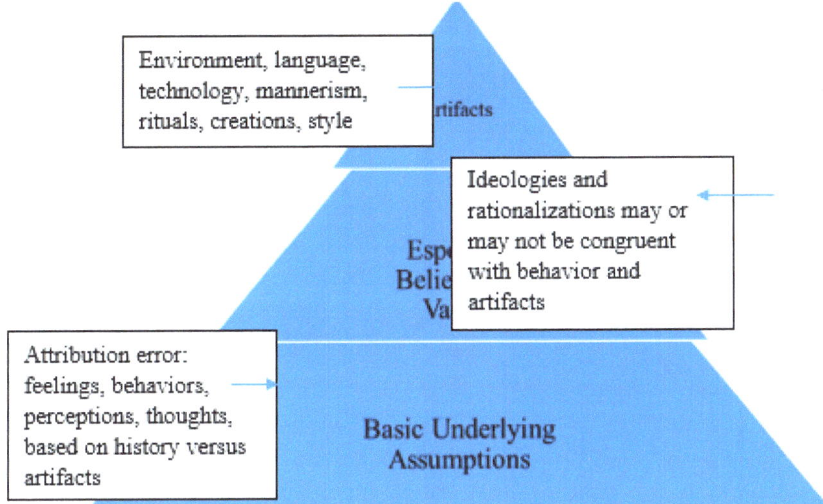

Figure 6b. Layers of culture pyramid

Culture competence yields culture agility

Chapter 3 explains the importance of empathy as a leadership-coaching competency. Empathy makes it possible for leadership coaches to express empathy toward a coachee by being attuned to his/her cultural norms. Chapter 4 discussed the importance of navigating blind spots to garner a renewed vision on cultures. Accordingly, cultural competence is fundamental to navigating blind spots by attaining insights on what diverse cultures value the most. Moreover, cultural competency enhances personal insights to equip leaders to become culturally agnostic and work seamlessly in multicultural landscapes. Understanding the intricacies of other cultures allows coaches to see beyond their learned beliefs and values system, hence removing ethnocentric biases. Culture can be a palace when it supplies all the simple needs (structure, material, relationship, comfort, meaning, etc.) for the sake of everyone while it can be prison if limited to personal life experiences when partnering with others in global experiences.[256] This translates into whether culture is viewed from an individualistic or collective vantage point. Cross-cultural leadership encourages collectivism and denounces individualism. To that end, how do we neutralize cultural beliefs bias so that common perspectives underpin professional development and career opportunities for all despite culture of origin? Empathy and self-awareness provide the answer. They enable cultural awareness and, henceforth, determine one's capacity to assess situations from a common prism to balance the playing field and afford everyone equal footing.

Since coaching is shaped by culture, cultural competence is essential to a coach's capacity to lead in global expanses. Cultural competence enables alignment among disparate societies and foresight to recognize needed changes to capitalize on opportunities and ward off threats.[257] Culture is not about nations. Rather it is about social groups and ethnicities that manifest in societies.[258]

Attaining cultural competence, according to historical-critical analysis, is understanding the context inside a culture to effectively relate to norms. Social analysis is getting inside the prism of cultural norms to better understand why people behave in a certain manner.[259] Social cognitive theory considers EI to be a multiplier for acquiring cultural awareness/competency. Emotionally intelligent employees are more inclined to identify cultural nuances and adapt to their conditions to better align through creative performance to the demands.[260]

> *Public school teachers, principals, and superintendents will now be evaluated on their cultural competency, or their ability to understand and interact with different cultures than their own (law spearheaded by Senator Mamie Locke, D. Hampton). History and science teachers will be required to complete training in African American History.*
> —Published in *Virginian-Pilot*, June 30, 2021, "New State Laws Going into Effect July 1" by Korle Dean, Staff Writer, *Virginian-Pilot*

When leading across multi-cultures, it is incumbent on leadership coaches to discern between the four major culture types and dimensions. The culture types are comprised of hierarchy, clan, market, and ad-hocracy.[261] The dimensions of culture are power distance (PD), uncertainty avoidance (UAI), individualism-collectivism (IDV), and masculinity-femininity (MAS).[262] Both the culture types and dimensions are illustrated in Table 6c.[263]

Culture Types	
Hierarchy (Control)	Formalized and structured to exercise control with clear lines of decision-making, standardized rules and procedures, and accountability
Market (Compete)	Driven by the market or environmental factors; demands core values that are competitive and result-oriented
Clan (Collaborate)	More family-like where teamwork and mutual success are of the essence while employee's professional growth is encouraged; mutual interest is paramount
Ad-hocracy (Create)	Innovation and risk-taking; where new opportunities are explored.
Culture Dimensions	
Power Distance (PD)	People separated by status where less powerful members of organizations accept and expect power to be unequally distributed
Individualism-Collectivism (IDV)	Shaped by how people are integrated to create success, whether communal or individual; individualistic societies often only related individuals to immediate group; collectivism societies are tightly integrated relationships of loyalty and mutual support
Uncertainty Avoidance (UAI)	Low tolerance for ambiguity; behavior guidelines, laws, and generally rely on absolute truth
Masculinity-Femininity	Masculinity promotes achievement,

(MAS)	heroism, assertiveness, and rewards for success, while femininity prefers cooperation, modesty, caring for the weak and quality of life; women are less assertive than men in masculine societies

Table 6c. Culture types

Traditionally, organizational leadership has personified the hierarchal cultures where relationships, for the most part, tended toward PD, individualism, and masculinity. These approaches are anachronisms to twenty-first century flat landscapes where people are more forward leaning with less division across ranks and genders. As well, PD impedes relationship building and promotes egoism due to limited communications between the leader and followers. Leading in diverse cultures requires clan culture which encourages collective employees' development and values the sharing of organizational wealth.[264]

Leadership wisdom fosters congruent cultures where the organization's strategy, leadership style, award system, employee management, and dominant characteristics are aligned to common values.[265] Once the vision is communicated, leadership's single-most cultural intervention is "wisdom." Wisdom states that the quality of relationships in organizations depends on the wisdom of the leader.[266] Overall, culture and leadership must be balanced and aligned for the organization to experience long-term success.[267] Achieving a higher level of success rests on vertical leadership development.

Vertical leadership development consists of developing consciousness and mindset evolution compared to "horizontal" skills development, such as communications and planning.[268] The key to increased opportunities and success in environments of rapid change is through vertical leadership development.[269] Vertical skills create lasting changes in the neurological structures, alters brain functions and worldviews, which enable more complex and nuanced intuitive thinking, feeling, and social adeptness.[270] These skills contain psychological capital that is a catalyst to developing the intellectual and social capital that manifest a global mindset and ultimately enable global citizenship. These manifestations result in leadership utilitarianism.[271] Global leaders' vertical development results in cultural agility that creates sustained performance in VUCA environments. Cultural agility allows leaders, owing to their multitude of competencies, to adapt to ever-changing conditions.[272]

Culture ingratiation accentuates culture competence and bolsters culture agility

Leaders are not born with the cross-cultural competencies that yield cross-cultural agility. Therefore, global leaders must be developed, shaped, and refined through cultural ingratiation from a blend of academia and hands-on exposure.[273] Because professors and students alike have difficulties escaping cultural norms, limited mindsets, and local practices, coupled with the conservative nature of academic institutions, the preparation to be global leaders requires hands-on experience.[274] Heightening cultural competence requires boots on the ground in global expanses to appreciate what each culture has to offer and to allow for the paradigm of cultural agnosticism to materialize and manifest as culturally agile leaders.

The greatest teacher of culture is experience as cross-cultural expeditions are ideal vehicles to develop global leaders.[275] These expeditions personify culture ingratiation which suppresses biases and involve getting inside indigenous cultures to gain a firsthand perspective on how they operate. A coach's cultural agility prowess is proportional to the amount of time she/he has spent in the trenches or experienced in the global commons.[276] Conversely, the less exposure one has to people who are different, whether racially, culturally, or religiously, the more likely she/he is to view other cultures through a narrow, biased lens.[277] Also, when a coach leads individuals in global cultures to foster a right-of-way to the other cultural ideas, new cultural norms can be constructed. This platform serves to illuminate the norms of the host nation despite the penchants of dominant cultures.

Is it fair and productive to impose ethnocentric behavior on diverse groups? As history has it, dominant countries are inclined to only see matters from their cultural perspective. When ingratiating with other cultures, dominant cultures, such as the US, must adapt to the types, dimensions, and principles of host countries. Naval leaders, by the nature of their global mission, have a plethora of multicultural training experiences but oftentimes fail to strike the right chord and establish an environment of trust, owing to ethnocentric behavior. The barriers encountered allow ethnocentrism to shape the interpretation of what they see at the deceptive, observable surface layer of cultures.[278] Assuming that other cultures are inferior because of artifacts, such as structures, technology, or mannerisms, can lead to miscalculations on how to engage and train.[279] Furthermore, owing to its dominant-culture behavior, the US Navy had a reputation for minimizing cultures of less-dominant countries, which leads to environments of consternation and distrust.[280] For example, when visiting other countries, it was common for Americans to have a presumption that everyone in the host nation spoke English. On more than one occasion, I was told expecting non-English-speaking countries to speak English was insulting and should not be a predisposition of Americans. Cultural ingratiation involves living inside the idiosyncrasies of other cultures.

Global leadership coaches must acclimate to the norms of those cultures they intend to impact if they are to be effective. In the book of Hebrews, Jesus went outside the gate to survey the landscape and connect with His people to better understand how to serve them in the church. This parallels coaches embracing other culture's ideas (global entrepreneurship) through firsthand experience to cultivate viable paths for success (global citizenship).

Successful global leadership coaches can build their culture competence through ingratiating themselves into other cultures. However, they must embody the requisite level of empathy and social skills to capitalize on these expeditions. The level of empathy can be enhanced through two concessions: (1) a temporary suspension of some of the rules of social order and (2) a concession to others' ways of doing things.[281] Additionally, coaches must be abreast of cultural dimensions and types and how they influence each society with which they are involved.

Again, this level of cultural understanding requires persistent determination of historical and social discourses. From both a social and historical perspective, the US Central Commander, while overseeing twenty countries stretching from Egypt to the Arabian Peninsula, realized that many Middle East states were only a generation or two removed from being European colonies or Soviet satellite states.

As a result, they lacked institutional enablers for democracy. This required him to advocate for more inclusive and participatory forms of government to strength civil societies.[282]

Conversely, if global leaders fail to identify with social and cultural textures, their efforts are stymied. Because national cultures are predicated on firmly imprinted values that are hardly changeable, global leaders' strategy must be comprised of methodologies that facilitate navigating sacrosanct landscapes.[283]

Stability is found in the sphere of being familiar with values, culture, and traditions that ground our society.[284] For multinational training, the Navy fosters this familiarity and creates a new culture between the two services by using both embedded and stabilizing mechanisms at the outset of operations. Prior to operating with Japanese and Korean Navies, cross-cultural training was arranged through port visits where social engagements, such as receptions, tours, goodwill events, or sporting events, were held. Then for secondary reinforcement, a structure or platform that consisted of cross-pollinating service members was arranged. US Navy sailors embarked Japanese and Korean ships and vice versa. The effectiveness of these engagements was dependent on Americans suspending ethnocentric tendencies. The engagements enabled relational competence, which develops both coaches and coachees through the quality of interaction.[285] Cross-cultural opportunities are made possible by cultural agility which is a catalyst to military operational responsiveness.

As for appreciating the social norms of differing cultures, I find it appropriate to look back at some of the actions taken during my engagements with myriad nations. I can't help but consider the question of why efforts to better understand approaches and means to embrace traditions and customs of less dominant countries have not proliferated. In essence, these engagements mimic global entrepreneurship methodologies of divergence, convergence, and networking.[286] Interacting with teams from disparate countries bolsters operational capacities through global citizenship. It is good to have a sense of culture awareness, but of a second order of value is the work to ingratiate oneself into other cultures to bolster and solidify this culture awareness through hands-on experience.

Participating in the teambuilding events with allied navies allowed the US Navy to garner cultural awareness and cocreate relationships before conducting dynamic exercises or operations. This is key to cross-cultural engagements because it inspires people of disparate cultures to work with the leadership coach to build a community of trust and be empowered to achieve a vision of faith.[287] Without this approach, suboptimal relationships would ensue, and diversity would act as a constraint instead of a resource multiplier.

Social intelligence—Community activities,
culture events, and cross-pollination

The following vignette are examples of Navy engagements replicating cultural entrepreneurship and cultural citizenship that I have personally experienced in diverse global environments.

Dating back to my maiden deployment to West Africa, I enjoyed the pleasure of visiting with diplomats to best understand the expectations and perceptions leaders had of the United States. One specific visit was when I accompanied my commanding officer on a call to the Senegal equivalent of the US Chairman of the Joint Chiefs of Staff. The Senegalese chairman, a general, shared a story of training at Maxwell Air Force Base in Alabama. I found that interesting as I grew up forty-five minutes from Maxwell, and now, I'm a continent away meeting someone who had spent time nearly in my backyard. Also, during a United America's Cruise to South America, I had the pleasure of being cross-pollinated into a Chilean ship where I was blown away with the experience of observing inferior technology as I observed the Chileans manually perform physics to obtain firing solutions on their weapon systems. The visit afforded me the opportunity to appreciate the culture of our South American partners and equipped me with insights to accommodate their efforts once I returned to the US ship.

It's best to listen to the language of cultures. Designing with other nations comprises using the language of host nation cultures so they will not feel as though their culture is forsaken; rather, it's integral to the solution.[288] I also enjoyed the firsthand experiences of working on board Chilean ships for integration and conducting collaborative events ashore with South Koreans to mitigate operational barriers.

All participants engaged in multi-culture teamwork must be integral to the learning process to garner trust.[289] Cultural awareness and trust are realized by getting out into the community. As the Commander of USS *Lassen* while conducting a visit to Shanghai, China, I toured several host-nation events in Shanghai that included acrobatic performances, financial centers, pearl towers, and their ships to better understand their culture and appreciate their national vision.

To remain globally effective, one must transcend cultures, or exude culture agnosticism.[290] Furthermore, to gain buy-in and implement a design that's palatable, global leaders must transform the minds of traditionalists by imbuing the coached nation with intellectual and social capital so that global leaders manifest as cultural citizens for the betterment of all.[291] Attaining global citizenship through cultural ingratiation is essential, but it must be an enduring process where its viability hinges on appreciating other's cultural norms, which is enabled through obtaining culture that's dependent on cultural competency.

Cultural agility

The complexities and vagaries of diverse cultures demand that global leaders embody special talents, skills, and practices. Moreover, leaders need to possess an expanded leadership repertoire[292] that enables them to adapt to multicultural situations without losing balance, which requires being culturally agile.[293] If one is to promote global leadership in a sacrosanct organization, she/he must design within the existing organizational culture, not for disparate cultures. This necessitates the embodiment of cultural agility. Cultural agility is an imperative as organizations require a pipeline of professionals of this quality to work in global environments.

Cultural agility is the capacity to rapidly change position without losing balance; the application of mega-competencies that manipulate cultural norms to achieve cogent behaviors of accommodating pretense.[294] Cultural agility enables technically competent professionals to be successful irrespective of the cross-cultural context.[295] This competence is predicated on the EI components of self-regulation, motivation, and social skills as they are key to transforming culturally agile leaders into culturally agnostic coaches. These attributes equip global leadership coaches with the social intelligence to envision beyond their personal values, associated groups, and life experiences. Cultural agility is complemented by culture competence and ingratiation as leadership coaches much get in the trenches to learn how to maneuver throughout disparate cultures.[296]

Becoming culturally agile is a practice that involves a process with three cultural responses to achieve success:

1) Cultural adaptation is used when adapting one's behavior the norms of the context and is critical
2) Cultural minimization is used when one's own cultural norms need to supersede the cultural expectations of others
3) Cultural integration is used when compromising adds the greatest value and proves well worth the effort[297]

Culturally agile leaders must have the presence to know when to minimize, integrate, or adapt when considering cultures is pivotal to effect cross-cultural, agile leadership.[298] They must understand cross-cultural idiosyncrasies to a level where they can astutely toggle between minimizing, adapting, or integrating with multi-cultures. A coach's cultural agility acumen is based on his/her capacity to toggle between the three responses.[299]

Culturally agile leaders transform global expanses into resource oases for the betterment of all. Human impulse is to internalize meanings resulting from cultural contexts. Alongside the impossibility of separating behavior from context, this internalization creates obstacles, requiring coaches to possess cultural agility.[300] The world is flat but replete with uneven terrain and potholes. What skills should global leaders exude to identify these uneven terrains and potholes to traverse barriers?[301]

Culturally agile leaders are distinguished by their psychological, intellectual, and social capital to think, create, and contribute globally. Nevertheless, their itch for continuous learning and keeping the saw sharp is pivotal. Cultural agility is an iterative process where global leaders demonstrate measures that allow them to effectively adjust to myriad cultures under varying conditions and circumstances.[302]

The viability of the process is predicated on a foundation of learning, which determines one's social class.[303] Social class, more so than culture, underscores educational levels and henceforth dictates one's latitude to drive change.[304] Global leaders must be transformational when engaging traditionally biased cultures.

Psychological capital, which is openness for a new experience and the curiosity and willingness to work across cultures, personifies this transformational leadership.[305]

In the grand scheme, culture is the refinement of the mind from both an educational and social standpoint.[306] Cultural agility is personified by global leaders who have the self-awareness to minimize their culture to consider the greater whole, adapt to other cultures based on conditions, and integrate with other cultures to add positive value through merging diverse cultural attributes.[307] The ability to discern between minimizing, adapting, and integrating relies on the personal coaching traits of the global leader.

Culture agnosticism: Product of ingratiation, competence, and agility

Adept global leaders are cultural agnostics, someone unwilling to commit to an opinion about culture.[308] Appreciating one's location manifests cultural homogeneity, so how does one overcome culture to realize agnosticism? Culturally agnostic coaches transcend their respective cultural values and beliefs to facilitate multi-cultured environments for the betterment of others.[309] Cultural agnosticism is when coaches are competent enough about other cultures that their respective culture no longer matters. They possess the aptitude to make decisions based on holistic cultural knowledge.

In this vein, culturally agnostic coaches must embody a passion for cross-cultural interactions which involve valuing diversity, fostering a common platform with those from diverse cultures, through interacting and seeing situations for multiple perspectives. Once again, the steady drumbeat is culturally agnostic coaches, who must be open-minded.[310] Coaches must keenly understand that one is unable to determine societies and cultures inside a nation unless they develop the interest to better understand the culture through exhibiting a global mindset, hence to realize culture agnosticism.[311]

How do coaches know when they are culturally agnostic? I would submit cultural agnostics solidify their state by taking calculated measures to not promote their own culture and suspend the thoughts that encourage cultural biases in the first place. The same beliefs that created blind spots must be abandoned. Signifying the confluence of cultural competence, ingratiation, and agility as depicted in Figure 6d, cultural agnosticism is dependent on demonstrating the same level of confidence toward attributes resident in other's cultures as those valued in your own. Doing so allows others to see your culture as being no different from theirs. They will not feel the need to minimize other cultures. This behavior is a matter of doing what's right for the greater whole as described in utilitarianism theory in chapter 4. Transcending one's culture requires becoming a cultural entrepreneur and citizen within other cultures.

Cultural Agnosticism

Figure 6d. Cultural agnosticism

In summary, transcending own cultures requires relinquishing cultural biases and not minimizing other cultures while embracing opportunities to adapt and integrate with disparate groups. Once coaches transcend their own culture, they are better prepared to make unbiased decisions that are removed from personal beliefs and values. Being culturally agnostic triumphs stereotypes and sheds light on values and culture characteristics that serve a mutual interest for the coach, coachee, and organization. Cultural agnosticism challenges leadership coaches to examine not only the what but also the why regarding behaviors and attitudes, rather than make assumptions about cultures. Becoming culturally agnostic is overcoming imprinted norms that are shielded by unconscious behaviors. This requires high EI leadership coaches to peel back the cultural onion to explore what other cultures can contribute to achieve OW.

This chapter articulated how cultural competence, ingratiation, and agility not only enable cultural agnosticism but also reinforce it to the degree where global leaders exemplify the capacity to toggle between minimizing, adapting, and integrating interactions with myriad cultures without viewing the differences as barriers. Although hands-on cultural experiences are valuable, the balance and integration of academia and real-world experiences are priceless for realizing cultural agnosticism. Fundamentally, cultural ingratiation begets cultural competence which begets cultural agility. The confluence of the three manifest cultural agnosticism, hence normalizing ethical behavior, beliefs, and human values. Leadership coaches aim to achieve cultural agnosticism by ingratiating themselves into other cultures, improving their cultural competence, and exhibiting cultural agility. This is critical because it represents the gap in behavior between the leader and aspiring leader who may hail from disparate cultures.

Although hands-on cultural experiences are valuable, the balance and integration of academia and real-world experiences are priceless for obtaining, refining, and sustaining cultural agility in cross-cultural settings. This is achieved by peeling back the onion down to the underlying assumptions and cultural values to shed new light on situations and opportunities that the global organizational alone do not possess the wherewithal to unearth. Regardless of their level of experience, global leaders must continue to seek ongoing self-development to refine their skills and renew their perspectives.[312]

CHAPTER 7
Empowerment through a Coaching Organization

Why did I choose to deliver this thesis? My leadership conviction has always surrounded the coaching methodology as depicted below in an excerpt from my command philosophy. I adopted this philosophy during my formative leadership years and continued to refine it as I became a more experienced executive. My model has always personified leading through people or leadership by the people rather than merely leading people. It has always occurred to me that leadership coaches should endeavor to produce future leadership coaches—the new themselves! This feat is done through a culture of empowerment which is enabled by a coaching organization. The organizational structure must reflect a SHRD design that champions the professional development and career paths of aspiring leaders such that they are qualified to become the leader's successor as projected in the *coaching triangulation* model.

> *My leadership philosophy is based on the coaching style. It's important that you communicate your concerns and ideas to me as well as others in your chain of command. I expect everyone to have the opportunity to grow personally and professionally. Reach out to your shipmates, up, down, and across the chain of command. Make each day a success by envisioning, persevering, and making a total commitment to excellence.*
> —Captain Simmons

Chapter 5 discussed the coaching conversation and how the coach and coachee develop a relationship of coequals to bring out their best selves. This chapter builds on the practices presented in previous chapters to cultivate a path to OW. By empowering aspiring leaders through a coaching relationship, *servantship*, five practices of exemplary leadership, and democratized leadership, OW is cultivated. The work discusses the benefits of a coaching organization and how to manifest a culture of coaching. Then it illustrates how *servantship* places the interest and professional growth of others above that of the coach by providing the requisite underpinning to buoy aspiring leaders to a higher state of well-being. Next, the chapter explores how the five practices of exemplary leadership not only empowers others but moreover facilitates their buy-in for organizational success. It wraps up by portraying democratized leadership as an elevated, flat platform that arms coachees with the requisite skills and learning opportunities to be effective future leadership coaches.

Organizational leadership hinges on fostering common grounds across organizations to afford a platform that equips everyone with opportunities to achieve uninhibited success. As such, global leadership coaches will benefit from the values and diverse perspectives of aspiring leaders despite the social inequities and cultural differences. This organizational benefit is achieved through establishing a coaching construct that draws out the value each entity brings to the team. The vision calls for an organizational design that transforms employees into coaching managers through a vision of shared goals between the coach, coachee, and organization.[313] Coaching engenders a coaching intervention that is, in turn, pivotal to developing individuals for increased leadership roles.[314] Coaching also facilitates strategic HR by assisting direct reports in attaining knowledge from experience to support long-term organizational talent management.[315]

One of the most pressing trends in today's leadership development is workforce empowerment.[316] Empowerment affords individuals the confidence, competence, freedom, and resources to act on their own judgment.[317] This realization is dependent on an environment that encourages continuous education, unlimited leadership development, and steadfast support. The ideal environment is fostered through elevating aspiring leaders to achieve optimal performance through *servantship*, which entails the leaders placing the well-being of aspiring leaders above their own.

How do you lead across diverse cultures and multiple generations in an AI-dominant landscape? What is the best way to connect to employees in a common plane so their views can be shared holistically?

The traditional leader-follower organizational structure has been preempted by congruent relationships. The saying "flat organizations" has become commonplace in today's work structure. I would submit that a flat organization is without merit unless those occupying the space exude the intellectual capacity and skills to inform decisions independent of positions. This coaching structure invites and encourages a culture of endless learning. Effectively, the flat platform must be buoyed by learning machines to elevate the capacity of the coachees to share a common vision with senior personnel. Coaches must embody the capacity to see across the organization. This structure marks a point of inflection for today's aspiring leaders where they are eager for increased responsibilities on day one and have a burning desire to influence the solution set.

Regardless of whether coaches are born or made, the principles presented in this chapter will ensure the development of high-caliber coaches. The principles captured in chapters 3 through 5 argued that once an individual identifies with his/her location, she/he can acquire the required skills to function as an executive leadership coach. The value added from navigating blind spots and the coaching conversations are matchless in preparing coaches of all backgrounds to be their best selves in myriad leadership environments. Although possessing innate intrapersonal and interpersonal skills is invaluable, refining and bolstering those attributes yield a formidable leadership coach.

How do you establish this viable coaching culture? When designing a coaching culture, actions must be deliberate and intentional. One of the objectives of executive coaching is to build a coaching culture to infuse a coaching philosophy into leadership and management style.[318] The overarching thesis suggests a coaching culture encourages everyone to aspire to become great leaders. It affords leadership coaches a viable resource to effectively perform amid disparate cultures by relating to everyone on an equal basis and from common perspectives. In chapter 3, I asked if EI skills developed or innate. Regardless, coaches can assist people with meager interpersonal skills to improve their levels of reflective, emotional, intuitive, and inspirational insights so they are able to effect change.[319] Coaching bolsters EI components.

Coaching advantage in organizations[320]

Coaching bodes well in global environments because the coaching platform personifies a flat and elevated stage for both the coach and coachee so they share perspectives on the organization's performance. The platform addresses both the pressing issues with leadership gaps and equips organizations with a blueprint to fix the leadership domain, extending the range across diverse global landscapes. Although coaching emphasizes the development of individuals, it serves a collective, second-order purpose of adding efficiencies and effectiveness to organizational performance and sustainment. Coaching enhances organizational performance by reinforcing human skills that are critical in a technologically driven, multicultural era. Coaching is preferred over consulting and mentoring because it assists leaders in expanding their vision, building confidence, and unlocking potential while taking practical steps toward attaining goals.[321]

As illustrated in chapter 2, coaching is used in the defense industry to develop diverse leaders through a continuous learning process. These leaders learn to adapt to elevated levels of change and to align cultures in partnership engagements in support of global security.[322] Coaching produces agile defense leaders and engenders trust among disparate groups. Agile leaders are key in environments of constant change where transformational leadership is pivotal to organizational success.[323] A one-size-fits-all approach to leadership is ineffective in diverse environments, so coaching must embody the flexibility to align behaviors as necessary to influence indigenous cultures.[324]

Coaching, rather than focusing on problems and addressing shortcomings, is positive psychology that builds confidence.[325] Also, differing from counseling, mentoring, and leading, coaching comprises coequals working together to highlight the untapped potential the coachee possesses while allowing the coach to advance his/her coaching intelligence. Mentoring can have an authoritative spirit that evolves from the mentee proclivity for holding the mentor in high regard because of the mentor's proven record of success. Counseling differs in that it rings a tone of negative connotation. The coaching process is inspirational in nature, which, in turn, allows the coach to tap into the coachee's innate talents.[326]

Coaching is the integral of leadership because it allows leaders to unearth and grow hidden talents that would otherwise not materialize; leadership is the derivative of coaching because coaching generates more leaders. Coaching equips coachees with the requisite underpinning to evolve from a follower to a leader by taking over the reign of their own future paths.

Coaching develops the self-efficacy necessitated by VUCA environments. It allows the generations who value immediate gratification to close the gap between where they are and where they envision being. Self-efficacy turns what would be challenges into welcomed opportunities.[327] Coaching allows disparate cultures to grow into one common entity of mutual values and beliefs. This unity is achieved through the sum-of-the-whole approach to leadership development by leveraging top performers to support the development of less-effective performers.

The process personifies leadership, expanding the individual form in favor of group concept; it portends denouncing the top-down model because "none of us are as smart as all of us!"[328] Coaching assists individuals to see inside themselves to see how their values align to their vision and for helping disparate organizations look beyond individual beliefs to coalesce mutual strengths. Emotionally intelligent coaches excel in global environments by using diversity to expand opportunities rather than relegating it to a constraint.

On December 21, 2021, a cohort member, who happened to be a former grassroots sports coach and now a current high school basketball coach, asked me why I spoke solely about coaching and disregarded leadership. I informed the gentleman that coaching is the new leadership model, owing to how this generation processes instructions and gauges authoritative figures. I discussed how the leader-follower gap had closed and training and development have morphed into a two-way information exchange of coequals akin to a coaching conversation discussed in chapter 5. Although flabbergasted, the coach agreed with my account.

The next section highlights the essence of transcending individual needs for the best interest of the whole—for example, coaching deontology. It introduces *servantship* which comprises both transformational and servant-leadership attributes. The *servantship* concept optimizes diverse values and infuses a sum-of-the whole approach for leading in global environments. This approach encourages collectivism that generates a higher state of being for individuals and their respective organizations.

Culture of empowerment through servantship sustains organizational performance

But don't act like them. If you want to be great,
you must be the servant of all the others.
—Matthew 20:26 (CEV)

Culture is more powerful than anything in an organization.[329] To realize leaders of a humble posture, organizations must develop a *culture* of empowerment and humility where aspiring leaders influence organizational successes. There is an element of psychological empowerment associated with humble leaders that results in a mediating role between humble leadership and organizational success.[330] The development of humble leaders amid this *culture* of empowerment must be underpinned by a fulcrum of humility that transcends the new leaders.

Establishing a *culture* of empowerment requires both servant and humble leadership that develops leaders from the bottom up unlike transformational and transactional that are the top-down approach to leadership development.[331] Leaders who fail to develop and empower new leaders merely surround themselves with followers.[332] Organizational leaders must be servants to generate greatness through—not from—those they influence.

Are coaches considered servants? Servant leadership is paradoxical because servants and leaders are opposites in that leaders drives matters from out front while servants excite/encourage the movement from behind. Also, the term servant leadership is troubling because servants do not lead, but, rather, they support the interest of others through positive influence. Considering this paradox, I coined the term *"servantship."* Considering servants help people improve their well-being by transcending their current position through infusing them with a new level of confidence to remove barriers, it is fitting to say a coach is a transformational servant. Elevating aspiring leaders emulates servantship, which entails being attentive to their concerns and placing their best interests above that of the leader—empowering them to develop their full potential.[333] It is my conviction that everyone should wake up each day and ask of themselves: "What can I do to make those around me better?" Chapter 2 describes the servant and transformational leadership approaches that merge into a collective, next generation which I have labeled *"servantship!"*

Servantship portends serving others to transform them to higher personal and professional status. *Servantship* pivots on empowering aspiring leaders to better themselves for increased opportunities. This empowerment is accomplished by positioning aspiring leaders on an elevated platform, independent of rank or position, so that they can see across the organization and share common viewpoints commensurate to that of senior leaders. Furthermore, servant leaders set examples through their actions.[334] A coaching culture of empowerment is ideal to accommodate those who are willing to sacrifice through *servantship*.

The seams between leaders and followers will continue to vanish, and servant leaders will become more transformational. Therefore, servant leaders and transformational leaders will occupy the same body. *Servantship* encapsulates transformational and servant-leadership attributes. *Servantship* is having a transformational impact through personal and professional sacrifices. It is far too often job seekers place undue emphasis on personal ambitions and too little interest in sacrifice…today's norm! *Servantship* implores others to step up and take on leadership opportunities. This approach extrapolates the greatness from the modern generation and today's knowledge-rich and innovation-intensive organizations that are committed to aiding followers in maximizing their creative potential.[335]

Considering organizations are adopting the flat operating structures, this position favors an elevated, flat organization. Of the culture types discussed in chapter 6, the clan culture embraces a collaborative learning environment where teamwork and mutual success is of the essence and professional development of all employees is paramount to the organization's overall success. In accord with this next-generation organizational structure, the subordinate role of followers has diminished.[336] As the gap between the leader and follower gets smaller, the leader is rarely the best and brightest person in the room.[337] Today's generations learn faster and have access to more information compared to older generations. Therefore, a culture of empowerment is essential to capitalizing on talent across all levels of the organization to underscore the integrated approach to organizational performance. This requires humility, which is not thinking less of yourself but thinking of yourself less.[338]

Empowering through five practices of exemplary leadership

Are leaders natural in their talents? Gifted leaders effortlessly resort to the five practices of exemplary leadership to oversee the employees' development and manage organizational performance.[339] Notwithstanding, it is incumbent on aspiring leadership coaches, if they are to experience an 80 percent chance of being successful, to model the way, inspire a shared vision, challenge the process, enable others to act, and encourage the heart.[340] Gifted leaders innately find satisfaction in magnifying coaches and extracting their best selves from within.[341] Successful change requires influencing others' perspectives, buy-in, and behaviors.

Model the way

Modeling the way requires coaches to ensure coachees can identify with this model through common relationships. Establishing common relationships depends on being able to empathize with coachees through being cognizant of their backgrounds and exhibiting selfless behaviors and leadership practices and measures. As someone who has led across myriad demographics with a multitude of trades and skills, I have always felt it was incumbent on me to learn the backgrounds to include hometowns, parents, siblings, industries, extracurricular involvement, and interests of each person to best relate to the cultures and values of each aspiring leader. As well, understanding the intricacies of their respective trades added even more valuable insight and afforded trust and credibility. My charge was to ensure that I was prepared to model the way through setting the right example.

Coaches exemplify modeling the way by marking the path through the example they set. Modeling the way involves removing barriers that could stagnate individuals or thwart the progress of the organization. During the Korean War (the Coldest War), Senator John Chafee instructed his marines to walk in his footsteps to ensure their safety so they could reach the desired outcomes.[342] Exemplary leaders must be credible by demonstrating strong values and traits, such as honesty, competency, inspirational fortitude, being forward-looking, and so forth.[343] Furthermore, the coveted leader must possess a consistent voice, magnetism, and charisma, set the example, ask purposeful questions, and act with prudent discretion. The model I portray is consistent with my organizational philosophy (being familiar with my philosophy is akin to being inside my prism), resident in my "Main Thing," anticipating, setting the example, and utilizing my values as my beacon. Modeling the way fosters a culture of excellence as illustrated below:

Foster a Culture of Excellence

- Adopt organizational philosophy
- Communicate the "main thing"
- Be forward-looking
- Lead by example
- Be value-driven

Inspire a shared vision

> *With every individual, there is a chance for differences in views. These differences may or may not generate change. In any event, when there is a possibility for change, there is a propensity for uncertainty. To lessen or alleviate this uncertainty, my philosophy provides the framework in which we will work*

> *with so that everyone will know what I expect*
> *from them and what h/she can expect from me*
> *as we work together to ensure Lassen is the*
> *most capable warship in the surface fleet.*
> —Captain Simmons

Everyone in the organization must have a shared view of the internal and external environments to readily respond to customers and outpace competitors. Leaders in PD cultures hold information as power and are reluctant to share with individuals of lesser status despite the fact they can make them successful.[344] Strategically thinking and acting on a common level requires everyone, regardless of position, to share a similar vision.[345] Creating a shared vision is more important to an individual's capacity to perform today than ever.[346]

Encourage the heart

> *Let us not grow weary while doing good for in*
> *due season, we shall reap if we do not lose*
> *heart.*
> —Galatians 6:9 (NIV)

Since I became an executive leader, I have posted the above quote from Galatians. Do not allow your position to mask (get in the way of) who you are! Encouraging the heart is a facet of a symbiotic relationship between leaders and employees, where high performance is elicited because leaders believe employees can perform the most challenging jobs,[347] and employees feel appreciated. This appreciation morphs into employees feeling valued, so, in turn, they develop autotelic personalities and become intrinsically motivated to excel at any undertaking no matter how challenging.[348]

Enable others to act

Do coaches empower aspiring leaders to act? If so, then how? Enabling others to act not only makes them feel like key players but it also portrays leaders as fostering collaboration and building an environment of trust.[349] Today's organizations are not linking strategic thinking to strategic acting, owing to old legacy hierarchal and power-distant cultural constructs. This construct is too rigid to pace changes in VUCA environments. Enabling others fosters ubiquitous communication among all levels of leadership down to the most junior employee. Everyone operates as miniature CEOs.

Empowerment enables others to act. The US Navy uses this approach when engaging partner navies, so they attain the capacity to act independently with increased responsibilities. This empowerment manifests from the situational leadership model where a continuum of leadership development transpires. Upward mobility is designed into organizational strategy instead of being happenstance.

The leader and aspiring leader relationship has evolved into a congruent relationship of coequals. Considering the miniscule difference in today's leader-follower relationship, this is good. This generation seeks more responsibility and aspires for empowerment. Empowering aspiring leaders requires a clan culture over a hierarchy structure; hence, the clan structure enables others to act.

Know Your People

- Interview coachees and engage their immediate supervisors
- Train, develop, and take care of your people
- Communicate your expectations
- Help your constituents achieve their goals

Challenge the process

Have a purpose that exceeds the status quo! This leadership practice enables growth and welcomes changes as no one has ever reached his/her personal best without challenging the status quo.[350] This practice leverages assessment and EI components. Challenging the process also involves moving away from the traditional leader-follower ethos while empowering those around the leader. This will require executives to take on risk as many leaders are uncomfortable with power and information sharing.

As a leader, it is key and essential that the process is challenged to foster an environment of genuine and authentic leadership. Authentic leadership enables an environment that compels the follower to share his/her perspective to create a greater common good.[351] Followers and leaders are two sides of the same process, so both are equally responsible for moving the organization in the right direction.[352]

In my experience, I find it critical for every team member, regardless of position or rank, to challenge the process. Otherwise, talents are not being fully utilized, and optimal solutions become elusive. To extract the best from team members, I encourage and foster an environment of critical analysis, creating thinking, independent thinking, an attitude of questioning, forceful backup, and mature thought-processing with second-order considerations.

Encourage Constructive Engagements

- Critical analysis and creative thinking
- Promote independent thinking
- Encourage questioning attitude and forceful backup
- Mature thought process with second-order implications

Once leaders acquire requisite transformational skills, they can exhibit exemplary leadership to grow new leaders by modeling the way, inspiring a shared vision, challenging the process, enabling others to act, and encouraging the heart.[353]

Empowering through democratized leadership

Every person will be his own CEO in the twenty-first century.
—Peter Drucker

Democratized leadership is a catalyst to leadership coaches sharing a common perspective on disparate cultures to develop global leaders independent of social identities.[354] It fosters continuous learning for all team members regardless of positions and roles. This continuous learning is facilitated in the clan culture which spreads intellectual wealth and builds diverse teams; it capitalizes on disparate talent pools.

To satisfy this colossal leadership charge, global leaders must possess the capacity to appreciate everyone's respective social identities by instituting a model for collective development over individualism. EI is the fulcrum to this collaborative environment of universal learning where everyone's perspectives are considered equally. The new organizational design reflects an elevated, flat structure. However, unless those who occupy the flat structure are learning machines, the structure design is fruitless. Continual learning is paramount to organizational personnel development.[355] This democratic coaching structure is the impetus to developing learning machines that will be the new HR strategic, imperative charged to leadership coaches.[356]

Based on research, it is fitting to argue that structure is underscored by organizational culture. Whereas hierarchal structures are less favorable to universal learning due to the vertical decision tree, flat structures inevitably promote a collaborative environment of information sharing.[357] This learning environment is dependent on a culture type that encourages learning across all entities. Of the four culture types—hierarchy, market, clan, and ad-hocracy again—the clan culture is deemed most appropriate for the coaching construct as it facilitates universal learning for everyone.[358] It encourages continuous learning and leadership development while advocating for shared success throughout the organization.[359]

Hierarchy cultures are discouraged because they are not conducive to information sharing.[360] Universal learning and continuous professional development are fulcrums to elevated, flat organizational landscapes. These flat organizations generate strategically agile coaches who are interchangeable and equipped to immediately respond to VUCA landscapes. Knowledge is only as powerful as the number of people who have access to it. In elevated, flat organizations, knowledge permeates everyone. The following are examples of how the elevated, flat structure contributes to democratized leadership:

- Enables a common strategic picture for HR development in one plan
- Engenders a broader vision for seeing over barriers
- Supports a scalable learning process to align to dynamic changes
- Encourages an organization of commensurate intellectual

prowess at all levels
- Enables transparency through open communications
- Facilitates learning and results
- Establishes trust

Trust enables sharing, which is critical to developing a democratic leadership environment. A climate of learning is created by people trusting one another as it is the only way they will grow and thrive.[361] Followers ascribe trust to the leader as the leader earns the trust through credible behaviors—transparency yields trust.[362]

Organizations must implement a leadership style to grow interchangeable leaders of commensurate knowledge. Collaborative environments foster synergy between coaches and aspiring leaders that enables strategic professional development in the same space.[363] Additionally, this elevated, flat structure creates a repository of knowledge or a learning incubator for the development of everyone. This structure supports reinforcing integrated thinking and acting while building like-minded team members throughout the organization.

The leadership approach involves the sum-of-the-whole approach to leadership development rather than a sum-of-the-parts approach. This results from executive leaders instituting an environment of transparency where information sharing becomes inevitable.[364] This information sharing engenders a culture of learning for which democratized leadership strives. Again, this leadership development methodology characterizes a collaborative environment that is encouraged in flat organizational constructs and, hence, is less favorable in hierarchal structures.[365]

When knowledge personifies power, it is only as powerful as the swath of people for whom it is shared. Therefore, an organization must share knowledge indiscriminately. One common challenge associated with information/knowledge sharing resonates in disparate cultures with varying views on who should have authority and awards.[366] The catalyst for information sharing across organizations is humble leadership coaches who not only admit to their shortcomings but also magnify the advantages and contributions made by their subordinates.[367] The humble leadership approach is unique because it focuses on leader's transparency about their trials and tribulations.[368]

The elevated, flat organizational structure is catalyst to developing a strategic working environment where the leaders and aspiring leaders can integrate seamlessly while manifesting an autonomous leadership development model.[369] This approach to strategic human resource development is a fulcrum to a culture of empowerment. Empowering others to act is pivotal to OW because it involves elements of OD and OS. Empowerment positions employees independent of assignment to an elevated stage so that they can see across the organization and share a common perspective with senior leaders.

Today's organization structures are based on shared learning and two-way communications where the delta between the coach and coachee is minuscule. As alignment between leaders and followers becomes more together, EI will become even more critical. Leaders will have to check their egos at the door and establish humble relationships with followers if they are to effectively influence employees of near-equal or compatible talents.[370]

For example, school environment now consists of open dialogue between teacher and students rather than the traditional lecturing format. They are now adopting teacher-student interaction approaches to lecturing rather than the traditional one-way lecturing construct. Open dialogue is more of an information-sharing construct.[371] Project teams are structured so any team member can demonstrate leadership rather than decisions being limited by the upper echelon members or project managers. All team members are expected to influence the process.[372] In parallel with coaching, shared leadership is a concept of influencing rather than directing.

Coaching is a lifelong journey of broad and influential relationships between coequals working to better the cause for one another. The coaching process has an element of reciprocity as the coach and coachee establish a dyadic relationship where the success of one is the catalyst to the success of the other.[373] A viable coaching platform has cascading and enduring effects for creating positive change for individuals and organizations.[374] Therefore, organizations must continue to encourage and adopt coaching to build an environment of learning to achieve optimal performance. This approach is key to reinjecting people skills into problem solving while imploring people to think for themselves while leveraging AI to pace dynamic landscapes.

Coaching bridges both AI and EI while offering an elevated

platform to navigate change and uncertainty. It affords a panoramic vision to span across confused environments to support timely and decisive actions. Coaching is a partnership of continuous learning to solve problems associated with AI and EI integration challenges amid constantly changing and uncertain environments.[375]

In summary, elevated, flat, and transparent organizations manifest from elevating employees to a higher level by empowering them through *servantship*, five practices of exemplary leadership, and democratized leadership. This chapter provided the tools to achieve OW through equipping employees despite position of qualification level, with the requisite tools to lead diverse groups in global expanses by highlighting the advantages coaching organizations create. By portraying how empowering others fosters a culture of CEO mindsets, the effort clearly underscored the value added from developing elevated, flat cultures.

This magnitude of employee development fosters high-level thinking across all entities to readily support VUCA conditions. High-level thinking and executive decision-making capacity are ubiquitous throughout the organization. This design suggests that future organizational leaders will feel comfortable surrounding themselves with leaders rather than mere followers as the biggest reward a leader can receive is the multiplication of leaders.[376] Organizations must develop internal entrepreneurs so everyone thinks like a change agent with the capacity to meet external demands on a moment's notice.[377]

PART 4
(ENDS)

CONCLUSION

CHAPTER 8
Championing Organizational Wellness

This chapter is fitting to conclude my doctoral scholarship as it codifies how I was able to leverage the first-hand experience of four at-sea commands and link it to my doctoral scholarship. This concluding chapter essentially formalizes my leadership coaching model by using academia to convey how to achieve organizational wellness (OW) through the applications of leadership-coaching theory integrated into real-world practical experiences. It is appropriate and worthwhile to note that the methods portrayed in this chapter are the same tools I used to successfully oversee top-performing maritime organizations where talent management was paramount to personnel and organizational successes. If developing successful organizations is of the first order, then sustaining these top performers is of the second order.

Why is it so often that organizations expend vast dollars on OD initiatives for them to only be short-lived? Perhaps, OD without OS initiatives is untenable for realizing OW. How often have you heard the cliché "the ends justify the means"? Chapters 3 through 7 illustrate how the means and ways interact in the *coaching triangulation* model to manifest the ends. In this chapter, I have strategically inserted the methodologies from these preceding five chapters into the organization design structure to provide practical applications on how the concepts facilitate OD and OS to manifest OW. Considering that the aggregate of OD and OS yields OW, it is prudent to approach OW as a dual-order process to perpetuate this high level of organizational performance. Along with equipping organizations with the requisite instruments to achieve optimal performance, coaching OW is also a catalyst to sustaining this high level of productivity regardless of the executive leaders' background or ethos. The framework is distinguished by its design whereas any executive can be inserted in the *coaching triangulation* model and achieve the same personnel and organizational performance results. This design was intentional to address the common problem of organizations relapsing when executive leadership changes.

This plug-and-play methodology is predicated on the interdependencies between the means and how they interact to filter the symmetrical ascension of the coach and coachee to achieve holistic success for the coach, coachee, and organization. Chapters 3, 4, and 5 presented the means that serve to fixate the locations of disparate groups while chapters 6 and 7 represented the ways (filtering) to cultivate the path to OW. The principles captured in the means and ways are what afford the capacity to insert any executive into the *coaching triangulation* model and achieve OW. Without the comprehensive principles illuminated in the preceding five chapters, OW would not be feasible. Those principles personify both the foundational and actionable elements to equip executives to successfully coach their organizations. This chapter provides how to apply these tools and resources and, in turn, highlights the leadership development mechanisms they enable. It reflects the end state by echoing the "so whats" of chapters 3 through 7.

Identifying with coachees' locations is pivotal to developing and sustaining impactful leaders. *Coaching triangulation* is pivotal as the design allows the coach and coachee to always know where one another is at any point of the walk. Integrating the means and ways enables and sustains symmetrical movement as coach and coachee aspire to move the organization to its performance apex. Reaching the performance apex reflects the efficacy of the aggregation of these leadership coaching techniques to cultivate an optimal path for an autonomous leadership succession plan.

Coaching triangulation develops new leaders by teaching leaders how to lead. OD excites the action to get the wheels rolling while OS keeps the wheels rolling. Although the mechanisms prescribed for OW are bifurcated between OD and OS, they can be blended within the two structures. However, the standard form prescribes strategic communications, *"Main Thing,"* and Strategic Human Resource Development (SHRD) in OD and coach-protégé program and intermediate performance reviews (IPRs) in OS.

Organizational development: Strategic communications "main thing" and Strategic Human Resource Development

One of the biggest challenges with leading disparate organizations is fostering a relationship of trust and understanding among the members. The first order of business is implementing processes to enact favorable movement for the leader, aspiring leaders, and the organization. The OD tools presented in this chapter encompass strategic communications, my *"main thing"* to set the standards for expectations throughout the organization. SHRD is included to delineate talent management principles to capitalize on human capital to optimally support OW. Strategic communications and SHRD set the stage for expectations and facilitate the development of aspiring leaders, respectively. OD involves the foundational tools that are catalytic to cultivating a healthy and progressive human resource culture. OD is critical to managing the efficacy of leadership development across organizations in diverse landscapes.

My *"main thing"* entails strategic messaging through communicating a singular theme to align expectations through transparency. The coach's philosophy is communicated so the coachee knows what to expect and how to execute the strategy. SHRD is distinguished from traditional HRD in that it perpetuates HR initiatives through adopting a broad and long-term view of how strategies, policies, and practices foster the achievement of organizational goals.[378] SHRD is two-pronged in that it affords a learning continuum and core-flex talent development models to underscore a dynamic approach to professional development to match the demands of global VUCA landscapes. SHRD is best when designed for both short-term and long-term planning initiatives. The short-term model would personify a two to three-year outlook on career development for a more immediate vision on talent management. The long-term consists of a five-year strategic outlook for career management.

Strategic communications pillars "main thing"

Communications, communications, communications! Communications not only help organization's members develop a shared meaning of ideas and events, but communications are also the organization.[379] As discussed in modeling the way, coaches must clearly communicate their philosophy, presenting an image of what is important to them regarding coaching inside their organization. Communication is key to accomplishing tasks, and leaders should spend a fair part of their day engaged in communications.[380] Communications are integral to establishing common grounds between the speaker and audience.[381] In diverse landscapes, coaches must be adept at reaching harmony, especially when similar symbols have different meanings.

For example, looking someone in the eyes in American signifies honesty while in some cultures, it is considered offensive.[382] Since my first chief executive job as junior officer, my top priority was to communicate my "main thing" to each sailor in the organization. I wanted to ensure transparency and make it clear that they had appropriate resources at their disposal to buoy their efforts and service to the command. I did not want them to have to guess my vision and use individual discretions to execute it. The goal was for everyone to play from the same sheet of music and keep a steady drumbeat. The messaging for the onboarding process was consistent across all positions/levels of responsibility and ranks/pay grades.

These pillars comprise responsibility, accountability, loyalty, and trust. They are my *"main thing"* to align my philosophy and vision for strategic communications to clearly define the key tenets to organizational success. These represent the pillars I value most and consistently reinforce as they engender transparency and facilitate a coaching environment where communications occur up, down, and across the organization. In this, everyone is empowered to act. Below is the introductory paragraph of my command philosophy which reflects who I am.

> *With every individual, there is a chance for differences in views. These differences may or may not generate change. In any event, when there is a possibility for change, there is a propensity for uncertainty. To lessen or alleviate this uncertainty, my philosophy provides the framework in which we will work with so that everyone will know what I expect from them and what s/he can expect from me as we work together to ensure* Lassen *is the most capable warship in the surface fleet.*
> —Captain Simmons

I also considered these four pillars to be the foundation to OW as they are integral to establishing and communicating expectations inside the organization. Personifying a communication nexus throughout all levels of the organization, these pillars have always proved critical to establishing worker-friendly environments of trusting relationships. From a macro perspective, responsibility and loyalty are opposites as the coachee is responsible to the coach to perform his duties while the coach must be loyal by being a good steward of his supervisory duties. Accountability and trust must be reciprocated between the coach and coachee. Both must hold each other accountable and foster a shared trust.

One of my former senior officers, a retired admiral, advised me to reiterate this message on each occasion that I was afforded to address the crew. This advice proved to be critical as it yielded brilliant results for establishing synergy with my aspiring leaders. The following paragraphs further expand on these pillars and how they apply to working amid disparate groups.

Responsibility (directional bottom-up). From the four domains of leadership strengths presented in chapter 3, responsibility, which is one of my top five, resides in executing.[383] Regarding my "main thing," responsibility characterizes the relationship of subordinate to the senior report. Subordinates must clearly understand it is their responsibility to carry out the duties as prescribed in their work description—this charge is inviolate. They must take psychological ownership of what they say they will do and demonstrate honesty and loyalty to commitments.[384] Furthermore, responsibility, along with honesty and loyalty, are instrumental values. Responsibility has been integral to my accomplishments throughout my career.

Accountability (bidirectional). Accountability is one of the most critical elements for fostering a collaborative work environment as people are motivated to cooperate and more inclined to exert effort when everyone is held to the same standard.[385] Accountability is not only the responsibility of the executive-level leaders. Junior reports must be charged to reciprocate this pillar to hold senior personnel to their strategic vision. Transformation takes place in organizations when employees hold their leaders and institutions accountable.[386]

Executives are expected to execute organizational visions and goals as communicated in their vision statements. Accountability comprises having a clear organizational structure in place that ensures responsibility for quality performance by employees.[387] Furthermore, the flat structure discussed in chapter 7 encourages a collaborative environment for which accountability is essential.

Loyalty (directional top-down). Loyalty captures the essence of a coaching organization. The coach displays loyalty by placing coachees in a position to be successful. Conversely, the coach can exploit employees for the short-term organizational successes if the development of the coachee is not considered with each assignment. Loyalty provides an environment of continuous growth and upward professional mobility by putting resources in place to support optimal performances. Loyalty has no place for the misrepresentation of authority and perceived power.

Trust (bidirectional). As posited in chapter 2, the rapid move into global interdependency through the virtual world makes trust more career critical than it has ever been.[388] Low trust slows decisions, blocks communication, and stifles relationships, which are organizational imperatives in global landscapes.[389] To tackle challenges and resolve conflicts, the relationships within organizations must be predicated on a high level of trust.[390] If a CEO is unable to engender trust among his/her workforce, his/her level of genius is insignificant because trust is the emotional glue that bonds people to organizations.[391] Trust is bidirectional and independent of rank and position in that it is equally important for the coachee to trust the coach as it is for the coach to trust the coachee.[392]

Oftentimes, senior leaders feel that trust is from top down, limited to them trusting their subordinates. One of my biggest pet peeves is that it is just as important, if not more, for the subordinate to trust the senior leader than the converse. I would always tell sailors, "It is just as critical for you to trust I will get the ship close to the pier to facilitate you getting the line over than it is for me to trust you to properly get the line in place." Trust resonates in action as there should be no light between one's words and deeds.[393] Trust engenders personnel development and organizational success. Hence, trust engenders loyalty, which is critical to long-term employee commitment and mitigates the risk of training your next competitor.

Career championing through Strategic Human Resource Development (SHRD): Learning continuum and core-flex program

> *If you stop learning, you will forget what you already know.*
> —Proverbs 19:27 (CEV).

As a career naval officer, one of the perks that enamored me the most was the premium placed on professional development and enduring education. During my initial assignment as an ensign, I can vividly recall sitting in the wardroom (the officer's dinning and lounging area) and reading through the Navy Postgraduate School Academic bulletin. After inquiring into why this bulletin was part of the magazine selection and later discovering the opportunities it afforded, I realized I had embarked on a promising and encouraging career. Additionally, the Navy always emphasized professional development opportunities, whether it was professional reading, leadership continuums, academic seminars, or job-related courses.

Because work environments consist of diverse cultures, eroding interpersonal skills, high turnover rates, and constantly changing external landscapes, professional development must be performed continuously by adept managers who possess a coaching capacity.[394] To match these conditions, coaches must continue to grow their bench by training and developing aspiring leaders to fulfill myriad responsibilities associated with work demands.[395]

Organizations must not only invest in formal education and professional development programs, but they must also formalize these processes by delineating explicit SHRD guidelines in employee handbooks. HR instruments, such as learning needs assessments (LNA), must be instituted to frame and govern these guidelines. LNAs involve a broad view of formal and lifelong learning requirements to pace changes. Formal processes comprise highly structured, off-the-job academic interventions while lifelong learning is driven by skill fade or merit amid change in technology or career demands.[396] LNAs must be sufficient to determine and prioritize the learning needs of individuals and teams to support short, intermediate, and long-term goals.[397] This approach to talent management is what truly discerns traditional HR from SHRD.

Organizational structure must be in place to ensure team members are being treated fairly while having a voice and the latitude to hold their coaches accountable. These structures are underscored by EI prowess, self-assessments, and navigating blind spots as explained in chapters 3 and 4. As a parallel to administering self-assessments, LNAs are equally critical to designing SHRD in AI-dependent environments where employees are keen on professional development.

They add immense value by allowing coaches and coachees to collaborate on deciding and prioritizing what training is required to meet new developments and technical demands.[398] As well, LNAs can be applied to strategically design career plans to identify education and professional qualification required for new hires to realize their potential and achieve job satisfaction.

Professional growth must be accelerated to keep pace with the dynamics of global leadership. Mid-level jobs require more education and knowledge where the middle class must work harder, participate in professional development, and attend to changing employment regulations.[399] SHRD must be intentional and consist of an explicit learning statement to communicate expectations for enhancing succession management and managing the organization's talent pipeline.[400]

The perennial conviction is SHRD must personify a continuous improvement process with a universal reach across organizations to capitalize on diverse values amid global expanses. SHRD should be a centerpiece during the formulation of organizational strategy rather than a peripheral function.[401] This strategy allows employees to envision their way ahead, which, in turn, makes success more palpable for the aspiring leaders and organization holistically. SHRD is best when designed for short-term planning and long-term planning.

Short term should offer a two- to three-year outlook on career development for a more immediate vision on talent management. This also bodes well amid the newer generations who thrive on tangible results. Career championing must comprise a long-term outlook of five years. Succession planning should be characterized as building the bench by bolstering talent rather than an end for the incumbent. Learning is a work of renewal, and it must become standard practice to avoid skill erosion.[402]

SHRD has taught me the value in developing the new me by empowering people through learning. What came first, talent or strategy? Talent drives strategy as there can be no organizational structure or strategy without creative and innovative people to lead new business opportunities.[403] The skill to develop people resonates in my God-given gift of teaching and perceiving where I can assess and act in a manner to realize new talent. If you want to empower aspiring leaders, you must know their position on learning needs.

I expect everyone to have the opportunity to grow personally and professionally. For that to happen, everyone must reach out to each other, up, down, and across the command. Everyone must make a concerted effort to make each day a success by envisioning, persevering, and making a total commitment to excellence.
—Captain Simmons

Learning Continuum. Learning is a lifelong journey. Individuals must commit to acquiring new competencies and knowledge that keeps the organization relevant and productive.[404] This learning pivots on leadership development that is characterized by the personal capacities to enable self-management, social skills, and work facilitation capabilities that support and inspire environments of enduring organizational performance.[405] It is the strategic planning of this enduring process that serves as the key to maintaining a roadmap for leadership development successes. Challenges faced along the path can come from myriad angles and forms, such as changes in technology, market conditions, or a shift in leadership paradigms.[406]

Organizations must approach leadership development from two perspectives: the level of leadership a leader innately possesses and organizational demands. These two perspectives are shaped by two actors that are internal and external. The leader's prowess is internal, and organizational demands are external. Coaching is situational, and the level of engagement depends on the location of the coach, coachee, and organization. It must reflect the amount of support or directing a coachee needs based on the level of experience and viability of embedded leadership development and preexisting conditions.[407] Employees with higher EI levels are better able to recognize and process information to evaluate their workplace position and identify with job security.[408]

Organizations must be mindful of embedded talent and expand leaders' capacity based on performance under routine requirements, external demands, and internal dynamics, such as successions.[409] This is done by approaching leadership as a continuum that cycles across four different stages, whereas each stage entails a different approach. Ken Blanchard claims that individuals progress through four stages of development, and each has a corresponding leadership style: directing, coaching, supporting, and delegating. The problem I have noted during many years of leadership training is these degrees of engagement are separated as though leaders are limited to one of the four approaches instead of applying them as a leadership continuum. Leadership or learning continuum is based on the situational leadership model where the situation characterizes a continuum across all situations, pending organizational and personnel needs. Developing a learning continuum requires applying these styles through the model of a leadership continuum which traverses these four stages of development.[410]

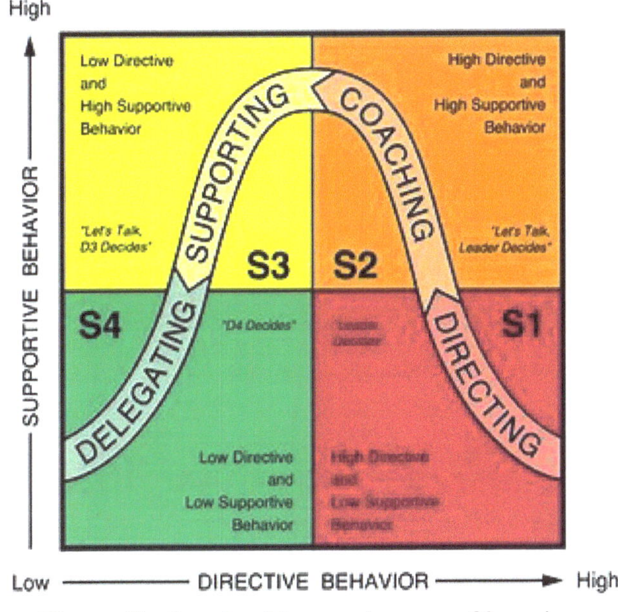

Figure 8b. Leadership continuum of learning

The situational approach to leadership is where the level of involvement with the aspiring leader is based on the leader-aspiring-leader relationship and the urgency of the situation.[411] Factors influencing the situation can also impact the motivation and capability of aspiring leader, the leader's perception of the aspiring leader, and the leader's perception of himself/herself.[412] As well, this situation can be predicated on time, the initial location of the leader and aspiring leader regarding cultural implications, social status, and values as discussed in chapters 3 and 4. I would submit that the more productive the cultural training is, the better the organization is at managing leadership development in diverse environments. The application of situational leadership can also help in bridging the cultural difference between leaders and aspiring leaders. Nonetheless, the leadership continuum must function across all stages of engagement.

The stages of engagement begin with directing due to vast difference in parties until more alignment is achieved. As adjustments are made and values become better aligned, leadership spends less time directing and moves toward coaching. In coaching two-way dialogue for verification and clarification takes place. As the team matures and the changes stabilize, leaders are doing more observing and supporting before finally delegating as the values reach a state of absolute harmony. As diverse (sustainment stage) values began to fully complement and compensate the strength and weakness of each other, the collective values take root. The process should be repeated as conditions and situations occur.

It is my conviction that to achieve efficacy in leadership development, the level of involvement should include measures to monitor progress. For example, as learning and facilitation are performed, coaches should model the amount of time expected to be spent at each level of involvement. Organizations should institute a methodology to move from one degree of interaction to the next based on qualitative feedback.

Core Flex. Just as I averred that a learning continuum must be strategic and intentional, organizations must design career paths for coachees from day one to ensure they are positioned to reach their true potential. The training and qualification requirements identified in the LNA must be prescribed through an agile process that facilitates multifunctional assignments to accelerate qualifications by performing jobs in parallel. I instituted this model during my tenures as a chief executive to catapult the qualifications and career milestones of the officers under my tutelage. This effort translates the process into corporate vernacular to champion the careers of aspiring leaders from their onboarding to senior leadership positions. As evident in the success of my understudies, the process is tried and proven.

The plans must be crafted in both short-term and long-term strategies to focus the coachee on intermediate goals and foster a strategic career outlook, respectively. SHRD leaders must be forthcoming and transparent with these plans to best champion success across all groups by way of race, gender, age, and ethnicity. Additionally, the strategic design must include equitable job and assignment opportunities. I make this point of emphasis based on personal experience where I was treated as an out-group entity—it was commonplace/routine for my promotion and professional opportunities to be limited. How often do out-groups hear that their performance marks or promotion opportunities are low because they didn't have enough responsibilities?

It has always been my conviction that success is the confluence of preparation and opportunity. The aspiring leader is responsible for the preparation. She/he must work tirelessly to acquire qualifications and credentials to position for opportunities. However, the opportunities are at the behest of the organization whereas it must have provisions in place to ensure opportunities are afforded to all employees equally.

The core-flex Process: Integrative and proactive training design[413]

Core-flex affords a viable platform of cross-functional training to facilitate a learning continuum, as learning is a lifelong need and people must continue to learn at all phrases of life both in and out of the workplace.[414] The integrative process uses a coaching methodology to champion professional development to expand human skills and manifest the requisite agility to adapt to external demands in an acutely competitive market. Although the process focuses on individuals' efficacies, it serves a second-order purpose to add efficiencies and effectiveness to organizational performance and sustainment. Essentially, linear and sequential training are insufficient to develop leaders to meet external demands. Without the intervention of this integrative and proactive SHRD plan, VUCA landscapes would be viewed as threats rather than opportunities.[415]

Integrative model of learning

This leadership development methodology includes an integrative process where employees learn their core skills while venturing into subsidiary efforts to grow additional skills so they can cover a broader spectrum of responsibility. The process is defined as core-flex merely because it facilitates cross-functional training to develop expanded skills. The model affords training in core skills while flexing to cross-functional training opportunities to enable integrative and proactive professional growth and development.

Core-flex is a bottom-up leadership process that hinges on empowerment of aspiring leaders using an integrated approach to training where cross-functional skills are developed by assigning peripheral training concurrently with core capability training. For example, the integrated training is structured in a manner where the aspiring leader's professional development opportunities are broken down into percentages. One month, she/he may spend 75 percent of their time focusing on core capabilities and 25 percent performing subsidiary skill development. However, the process is scalable based on individual progress and organization demands. Scalability mitigates risks associated with organizational production loss.

The process consists of moving individuals between jobs on a preplanned schedule to gain exposure and develop a broad spectrum of skills. It requires interdepartmental coordination between leaders. It involves assigning leadership coaches to each aspiring leader to track progress and adjust schedules for cross-functional training opportunities based on tangibly tracked progress. Core-flex reflects a partnership that requires quantitative and qualitative feedback and information exchange between the leader and aspiring leader through a coaching construct.[416]

Organizational sustainment: Coach-protégé program and intermediate performance review

The OD tools presented at the beginning of this chapter are methodologies required to excite this movement and funnel the course of aspiring leaders. However, OS is a second-order tool for pacing the movement and compensating for impediments along the path to OW. OS keeps OD efforts in play by "keeping the ball rolling," if you will. Initiating the movement comprises the foundational tools that are catalytic to cultivating a fruitful and progressive human resource culture. Sustainment of this culture necessitates ongoing human capital management initiatives to facilitate and champion professional development through a system of encouragement and accountability.

These HR management initiatives are resident in coach-protégé and IPR programs as they are the vehicles that personify the support structure highlighted in the fourth part of the coaching conversation as illustrated in chapter 5. These vehicles emphasize a dynamic career-championing process to support career advancement by leveraging in-house expertise and receiving near real-time feedback to enable transparency. There are no surprises as aspiring leaders know exactly where they are by way of performance and career opportunities.

Coach-protégé program

Twentieth-century HR practices observed hierarchal relationships, but twentieth-first-century practices personify an elevated, flat construct that places undue focus on the success of individuals.[417] This progressive structure affords HR leaders an ideal coaching platform to foster balanced SHRD across a diverse group of employees. Having a coach at one's disposal is pivotal because no one can reach his/her full potential without the proper encouragement, support, and guidance. Furthermore, no one is as smart as everyone, so good leaders foster collaboration.[418]

These personnel development efforts portend persistent career championing through a SHRD model that involves a coach-protégé program to accentuate coachee-and-organization performance. The coach-protégé program is responsible for career championing which, in turn, yields ongoing success for the aspiring leader and organization alike, further solidifying the distinction between SHRD from HRD.

> *Mentoring is best when it closely mimics coaching as it is not about imposing actions on mentees but rather affording a platform to draw out their best selves by allowing them to see what makes sense from their perspective.*
> —Personal conversation with Dennis Florence

Although my personal leadership attributes revealed in self-assessments indicate that I embody a formidable coaching repertoire, I have learned that coaches must continue to be coached for further development to meet the demands of global leadership. The best tool for learning is the counsel of others through vehicles, such as coach-protégé interventions. Also, the coach-protégé program is invaluable for accelerating the development of internal coaches to realize a coaching organization in a timely fashion. Coach-protégé interventions flatten and normalize disparate backgrounds.

Globality Inc.'s Chief Customer Officer, Yuval Atsom, stated, "A more inclusive workplace leads to better talent as those born with less privilege are inclined to work harder for opportunity." In this vein, the coach-protégé program I have instituted encourages interaction between different demographic groups across social and educational lines. To optimize universal growth, I have always employed interdepartmentally, interculturally, and across varying skill levels to best leverage talent, defy preconceived views of individuals, and suppress any stereotypical behaviors. As someone who has been subjected to these conditions, I felt it would be invaluable to share my experience and enlighten leadership coaches on how to mitigate these conditions through a coach-protégé initiative. I ensured mentors didn't default to those for whom aspiring leaders were comfortable or someone with whom they interacted within their standard reporting structure. The effectiveness of the program was driven by ensuring both coaches and coachees could manage to get comfortable being uncomfortable.[419]

In chapter 4, I described in-group and out-group relationships and how decision ethics are biased toward in-groups. To further expand on this thesis, in-group collectivism, which is the degree to which people express pride, loyalty, and a bond to their respective organizations, involves a group of senior leaders who make it difficult to enact universal approaches to professional opportunities.[420] So asking for change to the organization culture is akin to asking senior employees to divest in themselves and invest in someone different. Wisdom portends that a person grows rich not by what he has rather by that with which she/he identifies.[421]

Cross-cultural mentoring bodes well for mitigating in-group and out-group concerns and inclinations. As a leader of disparate groups, my modus operandi was to meet everyone halfway, regardless of their place of origin. Albeit the halfway point may require me to travel a little further to reach those who came from socially challenged or desolate beginnings. Regardless of their current location, I understood the importance of motivating aspiring leaders to take that first step or align their vision with the arch of advancement. People are encouraged by personal growth, achievement, responsibility, advancement, and inviting work, which all act as the impetus for upward mobility.[422]

A coach-protégé program which resonates in the coaching conversation must spread throughout the organization and implore leadership coaches to engage aspiring leaders from disparate ethical groups to facilitate diverse engagements to foster cultural integration. I made this coach-protégé modeling standard protocol. This bonding solidifies when coaches advocate for their protégés during meetings as it empowers them in the present of key organizational entities.[423] In addition to culture differences, coaching must transpire across five generations.

Intergenerational coaching is pivotal because it establishes a symbiotic relationship that enables growth for both the old and new generations. This transpires when older mentors share their advanced competencies with the less experienced protégé, while the coach also garners ideas on the application of next-generation technologies to expand their credentials for continued professional growth.[424] Considering re-skilling is common in today's workforce, LNAs must be performed consistently to facilitate short-term and long-term education and training needs to meet employee's demands.[425]

As an out-group member, it was commonplace for me to champion my own career cause as the strategic development plan did not provide provision for out-group entities. I was once blatantly told by my reporting senior that I was not a person he had interest in. Championing my own career prevented performance reviews from morphing into counseling sessions rather than highlighting my performance successes and designing a plan for continued professional development. I always found it hard to receive feedback on my performance or receive candid counsel when I was not doing well until it was time for performance appraisal. Performance appraisals should be about what's required to improve or further define your path to success. Negative counsel about what you did not do should take place during intermediate performance reviews.

Coaching programs are most powerful for developing multifaceted leaders when the coach-protégé dyad does not share common traits, experiences, and backgrounds as the differences allows the protégé behavior to be interpreted through different lenses.[426] Coaching involves a lifelong relationship of continuous growth for the coach, the coachee, and the organization through developing new leaders with the requisite skills to succeed incumbent leaders.[427] The coach-protégé program must deliberately ensure the right fit when assigning partners as the single-most important factor of success is the relationship between the coach and coachee.[428]

Is the right fit one of comfort or one which affords the best learning opportunities and facilitates the suppression of blind spots to increase culture competence? I would suggest that the appropriate fit is not a matter of being comfortable. In the coach-protégé programs that I have administered, the fit considered several key values to include differences in culture, social technical skills, maturity, and time in the organization. Assigning with regard to values for balance to capitalize on strengths and weakness to reach optimal performance proved viable. For example, marrying up someone who is good at speaking and presentation skills with someone who is masterful at collecting and analyzing data, but doesn't care to present, added value for the overall development of both individuals.

Assigning coaches in global landscapes must be done in accord with diverse skill sets socially, generationally, culturally, and ethically to maximize diverse values.[429] If I felt someone needed to gain a better appreciation for other cultures, I intentionally aligned the program to assist their growth in this area. When leading among disparate groups, leadership coaches must be careful not to default at doing what is comfortable.

Intermediate performance reviews (IPRs): Closed-loop filters for performance monitoring and facilitating and learning results

Today's workforce, which relishes empowerment and immediate gratification, demands frequent feedback to know how they are valued and their position regarding future opportunities. Coaching organizations must institute filters to provide this feedback in a systematic manner to facilitate course corrections, incentivizing, and increased leadership opportunities.[430] The process must be encapsulated in the SHRD as part of the facilitating and learning process to champion the third and fourth step of the coaching conversation explained in chapter 5. This facilitating and learning results is best administered through IPRs. As a closed-loop process, IPRs provide requisite feedback to inform performance adjustments, realize short-term goals, and stay on glide slope for long-term projections. While integral to transforming aspiring leaders into first-rate performers, the closed-loop information exchange must be iterative and circular to align expectations and glean desired results.[431] The viability of IPRs is dependent on suspending judgment while empowering aspiring leaders to visualize course adjustments through their renewed self-awareness. Standout coaches motivate aspiring leaders through displaying empathy by sensing how to provide effective feedback to enable optimal performance.[432]

Strategic opportunities for professional development should be readily available and integrated into the IPRs. When examining the direction of the current work force, one of the trends highlighted was the criticality of timely performance reviews.[433] Desire for timely and immediate feedback is high among newer generations as they are more curious about their progress and expect transparency on their future opportunities. Therefore, as a measure to reduce employee turnover, SHRD must be crafted with IPRs integrated into the plan.

IPRs provide an opportunity to take a position fix to determine location and corrective or regaining courses rather than a surprise or time to administer counseling. IPRs characterize a coaching conversation to design a plan to success. IPRs personify periodically taking a fix to mark positions based on the coach and coachees movement, IPRs enable timely course adjustments to support planned intended movement. The end state or final review should never appear as a surprise, owing to the periodic positions and adjustments delivered through IPRs.

Coaching organization must resort to measures described in the coaching conversation outlined in chapter 5 to facilitate the learning and results process. This involves providing ongoing feedback on call to action to best support the coachee in his/her path to optimal performance and increased opportunities. This methodology consists of measures to improve performance and professional development through fostering an environment of trust between the leader and aspiring leader through performance filters being a part of the SHRD. The Navy implemented a process referred to as midterm counseling to underscore this initiative. However, this system must be used objectively and involve candid guidance. It is only as good as the input of those who govern the process. Providing candid feedback on performance is a key enabler as it builds trust and encourages openness.

Moreover, IPRs are SHRD imperatives because they serve as a vehicle and barometer for assessing EI components. IPRs are critical because they

- afford a viable platform to mark progress (LNAs pertain) along the path cultivated in the SHRD to help coaches assist coachees with course corrections in changing environments,
- afford a preliminary look at and into how one is fairing in periodic performance reviews so that the coachee is never surprised or incredulous regarding how well or how badly they are performing,
- avoid attribution errors,
- foster symmetrical movement while taking periodic position fixes, and
- make annual performance reviews objective rather than subjective as the coach and coachee have synergy.

Therefore, it is incumbent on the coach to entertain this proceeding in an open and candid forum. Furthermore, in a coaching organization where locations are known, there should not be any attribution error (daylight) between the coach and coachee perspectives on strengths and weaknesses. These fixes preclude a surprise ending when it's time for annual or periodic performance reviews. Reviews should never morph into counseling sessions if the coach and coachee are on the same page and share a trusting relationship. Feedback builds trust, and coaches are charged to accompany aspiring leaders during the development process.

IPRs deepen self-awareness, and self-aware individuals know and are comfortable talking about their limitations and strengths.[434] Feedback is an HR imperative for performance improvement and adaptability when developing new coaches.

Gallup researchers found that good managers are not bosses, they are coaches. These coaches focus on individual and team strengths and setting clear expectations and performance goals while offering feedback that optimizes individual strength and increases team effectiveness.[435] When administered appropriately, IPRs replicate this behavior and provides coachees an update (GPS) on their progress. Great coaches consistently seek feedback for process improvement.

President Carter said he would ask questions of his audience after each speaking engagement as a measure to solicit feedback and would apply this feedback to inform his next speaking event.[436] Feedback facilitates the call to action and supports facets of the coaching conversation. Accordingly, feedback should be continuous through career championing programs, such as coach-protégé and SHRD plans, to afford real-time course adjustments. These programs should be melded into the coaching conversation, specifically the call to action and supporting steps. IPRs provide timely filtering for short-term SHRD to inform immediate course adjustments while long-term SHRD measures support more strategic career projections. The short-term performance filters must involve open-ended discussion and intuitive listening to draw out call-to-action performance improvements in the near term.

I always graded aspiring leaders more austerely during the IPR so they would aim higher or walk a compensating course to overcome impediments to arrive at the position envisioned or to better align them to their trajectory for success. If IPR systems are administered appropriately, it allows the coachee to improve upon his processes and demonstrate improvement between the session and the actual performance setting. As well, the respective coach participates in these IPRs for accountability and to reinforce the integrity of the coach-protégé program.

SHRD starts on day one and lessens turnovers through strategic HR engagements. Assessments are day-one imperatives to determine the strategic direction of the coachee. The fitting question is, does a different conversation transpire between in-groups and out-groups? This harkens back to normalizing cultural differences as addressed in chapters 4 and 6. The forum should invite open dialogue despite group affiliation, which reflects being culturally agnostic. Aspiring leaders should not be surprised to learn they are not on glide slope for career milestones—how well or poorly they are performing should never occur as a surprise.

It is important to note that the third step in the coaching conversation is a call to action while the fourth step is to support the action. This support is administered through feedback mechanisms, such as IPRs. Aspiring leaders should not be surprised about their performance as the feedback should be akin to that offered when supporting the call to action. The IPRs mimics the facilitating and learning measures illustrated in chapter 5. It is far too often that I speak with aspiring leaders in myriad professions, only to discover they are not apprised on how they are performing and they are uninformed about the strategic outlook for their upward mobility/career opportunities. These conditions highlight why IPRs are viable platforms to discuss and design long-term professional development, and potentially conduct LNAs, as warranted. These plans of actions and milestones (POA&M) should be resident in aspiring leaders' SHRD plans as part of learning and facilitating to ensure support is in place to champion career development across all groups.

From personal experience, IPRs are oftentimes a sticking point when you are not part of the in-group as career information is privy to those with whom the coach has more in common and for whom the coach is more willing to promote career needs. Career championing was not favorable to out-groups as it disrupted career opportunities for in-group strategic career plans.

Oftentimes, cultural and generational differences can preclude openness, owing to not having empathy and self-awareness regarding expectations of out-groups. To further expound, communications between coach and coachee for out-groups are insufficient to improve the self-awareness of the coach regarding the professional needs of the coachee. If the leader and aspiring leader are not connected socially, then this becomes a challenge of "what is appropriate that we ought to talk about openly." The ought-self pales to the want-self due to leaders not being comfortable sharing valuable information with out-groups and not recognizing out-groups deserve to have essential information at their disposal for uniform growth. Because of leaders' proclivity to be uncomfortable being candid with those with whom they are unable to connect, navigating blind spots and the coaching conversations are needed to mitigate these behaviors.

In my personal experience, obtaining objective feedback on my performance and securing career championing were met with the most austere challenges. The underlying issues can surround open dialogue if social identities between the leader and aspiring leader are not flattened. As well, leaders are reluctant to provide candid feedback to those (out-groups) within whom they are not familiar for fear of offending them. This dilemma likely stems from not knowing the location of the aspiring leader. My experience was replete with these barriers, which eventually led to leaders using performance appraisals as the platform to inform me of my deficiencies. This assertion is based on my personal experience of not being afforded opportunities for open and candid dialogue that should have manifested in performance appraisal reviews. My IPRs reflected a selective and careful dialogue that was relegated to a check-in-the-block engagement, owing to uncommon locations or group disparities.

Leadership coaches must embrace their responsibilities to champion the careers of everyone to whom they are responsible. Performance reviews are not a time to tell someone about his/her weaknesses. This was a common occurrence when my senior reports needed justifications to rate me low in certain areas or attempted to champion the careers of my counterparts. I have been told on occasions that I had to await my turn and my report was not based on performance.

The institutionalization and adherence to the mechanisms presented in this chapter will sustain organizational health regardless of leadership changes. The effects will reduce employee turnover through fostering a progressive talent management culture that involves universal career championing. This championing and sustainment of organizational performance is highlighted by the systemic approach to SHRD that leverages a coaching culture to achieve OW. Retention is improved by promoting deliberate and intentional talent development throughout the organization independent of social status.

Coaching in organizations allows expanded business views and engagements because it grows a deep bench of talent capable of performing interchangeably.[437] The risks and consequences of not implementing strategic communications, SHRD, coach-protégé programs, and IPRs are plain; executives will spend an inordinate amount of time replacing talent at the end of performance cycles.

Championing OW stays to the left or out front of these unwanted occurrences by walking alongside aspiring leaders and marking their every step to success.

ABOUT THE AUTHOR

Dr. Anthony L. Simmons is a retired navy captain who served twenty-eight years as a surface warfare officer. His navy experience consisted of four at-sea commands: a patrol coastal, two Aegis destroyers, and a destroyer squadron. Ashore, he worked in human resources at the Navy Bureau of Personnel and the Pentagon on the staffs of the chairman of the Joint Chiefs and naval operations as a strategic planner and resource officer. He currently works in the maritime defense sector. He holds a doctorate degree in strategic leadership from Regent University, a master's in mechanical engineering from Naval Postgraduate School, a master's in military operational art and science from Air University, and a bachelor's degree in robotics from Austin Peay State University. Dr. Simmons grew up in the rural, working-class town of Goodwater, Alabama, where he graduated from Goodwater High School in 1985 as valedictorian, was honored as an all-state football player, and earned a full football scholarship to Austin Peay. Dr. Simmons is the founder and owner of Sixth Gear Consulting, LLC, which is a leadership performance consulting practice that instructs leaders on how to lead through bridging people and technology.

http://www.sixthgearconsulting.com/

REFERENCES

[1] Hunt, J. M. and Weintraub, J. R. 2007. *The Coaching Organization: A strategy for developing leaders.* Sage.

[2] Palmer, S. and Whybrow, A. 2019. *Handbook of Coaching Psychology.* Routledge.

[3] Hunt, J. M. and Weintraub, J. R. 2007. *The Coaching Organization: A strategy for developing leaders.* Sage.

[4] Changeboard Team. November 27, 2012. The evolution of coaching. *Changeboard.* Retrieved from https://www.changeboard.com/article-details/13946/the-evolution-of-coaching/.

[5] Changeboard Team. November 27, 2012. The evolution of coaching. *Changeboard.* Retrieved from https://www.changeboard.com/article-details/13946/the-evolution-of-coaching/.

[6] Changeboard Team. November 27, 2012. The evolution of coaching. *Changeboard.* Retrieved from https://www.changeboard.com/article-details/13946/the-evolution-of-coaching/.

[7] Goleman, D. 2011. What makes a leader? In *HBR's 10 must reads on leadership.* (pp. 1–22). Harvard Business Review Press.

[8] Hunt, J. M. and Weintraub, J. R. 2007. *The Coaching Organization: A strategy for developing leaders.* Sage.

[9] Cunningham, K. J. January 7, 2020. How to Triangulate Your Position on a Map Accurately. *My Open Country.* Retrieved from https://www.myopencountry.com/how-to-triangulate-map/.

[10] Yarger, H. R. 2008. Toward a theory in strategy: Art Lykke and the US Army War College strategy model. *US Army War College guide to national security issues,* 1, 44–47.

[11] Bazerman, M. H. and Tenbrunsel, A. E. 2011. *Blind Spots.* Princeton University Press.

[12] Blackbyrn, A. January 15, 2020. The Coach Accelerator [Webinar]. *In LLC Webinar Series.* Retrieved from https://events.genndi.com/lve/818182175026321098/378fdd5704/jot/173149392.

[13] Collins, G. R. 2009. *Christian Coaching: Helping Others Turn Potential into Reality.* NavPress.
Stoltzfus, T. 2005. *Leadership coaching: The disciplines, skills and heart of a Christian coach.* NavPress.

[14] Hunt, J. M. and Weintraub, J. R. 2007. *From The Coaching Organization.* Sage, pp. 1–3.

[15] Collins, G. R. 2009. *Christian Coaching: Helping Others Turn Potential into Reality.* NavPress, p. 315.

[16] Hicks, R. and McCracken, J. 2011. Coaching as a leadership style. *Physician Executive,* 37(5), 70.

[17] Kampa-Kokesch, S. and Anderson, M. Z. 2001. Executive coaching: A comprehensive review of the literature. *Consulting Psychology Journal: Practice and Research,* 53(4), 205–228.

---

18 Palmer, S. and Whybrow, A. 2019. *Handbook of Coaching Psychology*. Routledge.

19 Stoltzfus, T. 2005. *Leadership coaching: The disciplines, skills and heart of a Christian coach*. NavPress.

Goleman, D. 2011. What makes a leader? In *HBR's 10 must reads on leadership*. (pp. 1–22). Harvard Business Review Press.

20 Stoltzfus, T. 2005. *Leadership coaching: The disciplines, skills and heart of a Christian coach*. NavPress.

21 Kimsey-House, H., Kimsey-House, K., Sandahl, P., and Whitworth, L. 2018. *Co-Active Coaching*. Nicholas Brealey.

22 Stoltzfus, T. 2005. *Leadership coaching: The disciplines, skills and heart of a Christian coach*. NavPress.

23 Northouse, P. G. 2013. *Leadership Theory and Practice*. Sage, p. 99.

24 Northouse. 2013. p. 219.

25 Northouse. 2013. p. 186.

26 Crane, T. G. 2017. *The heart of coaching: Using transformational coaching to create a high-performance culture*. FTA Press, p. 31.

27 Mihiotis, A. and Argirou, N. 2016. Coaching: From challenge to opportunity. *Journal of Management Development*, 35(4), 448–463.

28 Stoltzfus, T. 2005. *Leadership coaching: The disciplines, skills and heart of a Christian coach*. NavPress.

29 Rath, T. 2008. *Strengths based Leadership*. Gallup Press, p. 23.

30 Collins, G. R. 2009. *Christian Coaching: Helping Others Turn Potential into Reality*. NavPress.

Stoltzfus, T. 2005. *Leadership coaching: The disciplines, skills and heart of a Christian coach*. NavPress. Christian Coaches Network International and International Coach Federation (2017). Retrieved from https://christiancoaches.com/wp-content/uploads/2017/10/Competencies-Edited-Final-2017.pdf.

31 Dingman, W. W. 2006. Servant leadership's role in the succession planning process: A case study Retrieved from
http://regent.summon.serialssolutions.com/2.0.0/link/0/eLvHCXMwrV1NS8NAEB1q60E8qKio1bI3T6nJJtlkBRE_WqUHqVJa9VKS_UBB0tra_-_OdlPFiiePSwgkO7tvZvfNzAMIadP3fmBCILgOKZdURkEUqIzGmTbLi2ZKUlQYQWamHw-ew_4jbVegW5bGOHOXKGmhW44E3pqflEGEzVro-fjdQxkppFtLTY3MaS3lM1sruQI1BGvM-UoGT78d52MLzDxirivPYrwE0tbztDegzD1T5lzcnCishFpqhet6Ov7nr2zC-vU3qn4LKqrYhg5Ci7EFeVtkQB9PCWYokteCmFiSTGdWgdG8QsZOD4mM58Ulp-SCCOM0iW1puwO9dqt3des5NQbvxXycp02oJUPjzXksfC5SnTJFE6pZEuV5HvNU8lgHSU61LznPNfU1EyKOzMndRARMhbtQLUaF2gMiwsxYP0hlqC1NmzGULmISKUqMAPehXs7S0O2o6XAxRQd_Pq3D2tclySFUPyYzdQSrc_M0YMXv3DfsGmhA7bJ1130woxvqfwIK4sdW.

32 Phillips, T. 2011. Creating a coaching culture across a global sales force. *Strategic HR Review*, 10(4), 5–10.

REFERENCE

[33] Crane, T. G. 2017. *The heart of coaching: Using transformational coaching to create a high-performance culture*. FTA Press.

[34] Amanchukwu, R. N., Stanley, G. J., and Ololube, N. P. 2015. A Review of Leadership Theories, Principles and Styles and Their Relevance to Educational Management. *Management*, 5(1), 6–14.

[35] Watkins, D. 2008. The common factors between coaching cultures and transformational leadership, transactional leadership, and high-performance organizational cultures. Available from Dissertations and Theses at University of Phoenix (264; 3350860).

[36] Phillips, T. 2011. Creating a coaching culture across a global sales force. *Strategic HR Review*, 10(4), 5–10.

[37] Mitchell, N. 2015. *Phenomenological study of the mentoring behaviors of the four quadrants of situational leadership within the department of defense* (Order No. 3724514). Available from Dissertations & Theses at Regent University; ProQuest Dissertations and Theses Global; ProQuest One Academic. (1730385984). Retrieved from http://eres.regent.edu:2048/login?url=https://search-proquest-com.ezproxy.regent.edu/docview/1730385984?accountid=13479.

[38] Robinson, T. L. 2016. *Leadership coaching for new administrators using the blended coaching model*. Retrieved httip://regent.summon.serialssolutions.com.

[39] Passmore, J. 2012. *Psychometrics in Coaching: Using psychological and psychrometric tools for development*, Kogan Page Limited.

[40] Herd, A. M., Alagaraja, M., and Cumberland, D. M. 2016. Assessing global leadership competencies: The critical role of assessment centre methodology. *Human Resource Development International*, 19(1), 27–43.

[41] Dean, B. P. 2007. *Cultural intelligence in global leadership: A model for developing culturally and nationally diverse teams* (Order No. 3292256). Available from Dissertations & Theses at Regent University. (304713848).

[42] Stoltzfus, T. 2005. *Leadership coaching: The disciplines, skills and heart of a Christian coach*. NavPress, pp. 4–21.

[43] Goleman, D. 2005. *Emotional Intelligence; why it can matter more than IQ*. Bantam Dell.

[44] Chatterjee, D. 2006. Wise Ways: Leadership as Relationship. *Journal of Human Values*, 12(2), 153–160.

[45] Hunt, J. M. and Weintraub, J. R. 2007) *From the Coaching Organization*. Sage.

[46] Hunt and Weintraub. 2007. p. 15.

[47] Buljac-Samardzic, M. and van Woerkom, M. 2015. Can managers coach their teams too much? *Journal of Managerial Psychology*, 30(3), 280–296.

[48] Barton, D., Grant, D., and Horn M. 2012. Leading in the 21st Century. *McKinsey Quarterly*, 1–17.

[49] Mitchell, N. 2015. *Phenomenological study of the mentoring behaviors of the four quadrants of situational leadership within the department of defense* (Order No. 3724514). Available from Dissertations & Theses at Regent University; ProQuest Dissertations & Theses Global; ProQuest One Academic. (1730385984). Retrieved from http://eres.regent.edu:2048/login?url=https://search-proquest-com.ezproxy.regent.edu/docview/1730385984?accountid=13479.

[50] Mitchell. 2015.

[51] Stoltzfus, T. 2005. *Leadership coaching: The disciplines, skills and heart of a Christian coach.* NavPress.
Crane, T. G. 2017. *The heart of coaching: Using transformational coaching to create a high-performance culture.* FTA Press. International Coach Federation (2019). Retrieved from **https://coachfederation.org/core-competencies**.

[52] Perkins, A. W. 2009. Global Leadership Study: A Theoretical Framework. *Journal of Leadership Education*, 8(2), 72–83.

[53] Maxwell, J. C. 2020. *The Leader's Greatest Return: attracting, developing, and multiplying leader.* HarperCollins.

[54] Caligiuri, P. 2012. *Cultural Agility; Building a Pipeline of Successful Global Professionals.* Jossey-Bass. p. 5.

[55] Peláez Zuberbuhler, M. J., Salanova, M., and Martínez, I. M. 2020. Coaching-based leadership intervention program: A controlled trial study. *Frontiers in Psychology, 10.*

[56] Joiner, B. and Josephs, S. 2007. Developing agile leaders. *Industrial and Commercial Training*, 39(1), 35–42.

[57] Covey, S. M. R. and Merrill, R. R. 2006. *The Speed of Trust.* Simon & Schuster.

[58] Covey and Merrill. 2006.

[59] Kouzes, J. and Posner, B. 2017. *The leadership challenge 6th ed.* John Wiley and Sons.

[60] Perkins, A. W. 2009. Global Leadership Study: A Theoretical Framework. *Journal of Leadership Education*, 8(2), 72–83.

[61] Darby, R. 2015. Leadership development in the Asia-Pacific region. building capacity in the Indonesia defense environment: A case study. *Journal of Management Development*, 34(5), 506–523.

[62] Javidan, M., House, R. J., Dorfman, P. W., Hanges, P. J., and Sully de Luque, M. 2006. Conceptualizing and measuring cultures and their consequences: A comparative review of GLOBE's and hofstede's approaches. Journal of International Business Studies, 37(6), 897–914.

[63] House et. al. 2004. Culture, Leadership, and Organizations. *The Globe Study of 62 Societies, United Kingdom.* Sage Publications.

[64] Joiner, B. and Josephs, S. 2007. Developing agile leaders. *Industrial and Commercial Training*, 39(1), 35–42.

[65] Joiner and Josephs. 2007.

[66] Berg, M. E. and Karlsen, J. T. 2016. A study of coaching leadership style practice in projects: MRN. *Management Research Review, 39*(9), 1122–1142.

[67] Daniel Goleman. 2011. What makes a leader? In *HBR's 10 must reads on leadership.* Harvard Business Review Press, 1.

[68] Goleman. 2011.

[69] Caligiuri, P. 2012. *Cultural Agility; Building a Pipeline of Successful Global Professionals,* Jossey-Bass.

[70] Goleman, D. 2011. What makes a leader? In *HBR's 10 must reads on leadership.* (pp. 1–22). Harvard Business Review Press.

[71] Goleman. 2011.

[72] Collins, G. R. 2009. *Christian Coaching: Helping Others Turn Potential into Reality.* NavPress.

[73] Northouse, P. G. 2013. *Leadership Theory and Practice.* Sage.

[74] Northouse. 2013.

[75] Goleman, D. 2011. What makes a leader? In *HBR's 10 must reads on leadership*. (pp. 1–22). Harvard Business Review Press.

[76] Maamari, B. E. and Majdalani, J. F. 2017. Emotional Intelligence, Leadership & Organizational Climate. *International Journal of Organizational Analysis*, 25(2), 327–345.

[77] Goleman, D. 2011. What makes a leader? In *HBR's 10 must reads on leadership*. (pp. 1–22). Harvard Business Review Press.

[78] Goleman. 2011.

[79] Goleman. 2011.

[80] Goleman. 2011.

[81] Goleman. 2011.

[82] Goleman. 2011.

[83] Welch, J. 2001. *Jack: Straight from the gut*. Warner Books.

[84] Welch. 2001.

[85] Welch, J. 2005. *Winning*. HarperCollins.

[86] Reuven, B. 2002. *BarOn Emotional Quotient Inventory*. Multi-Health Systems Inc.

[87] Goleman, D. 2011. What makes a leader? In *HBR's 10 must reads on leadership*. (pp. 1–22). Harvard Business Review Press

[88] Welch, J. 2005. *Winning*. HarperCollins.

[89] Goleman, D. 2011. What makes a leader? In *HBR's 10 must reads on leadership*. (pp. 1–22). Harvard Business Review Press

[90] Goleman. 2011.

[91] Goleman. 2011.

[92] Goleman. 2011.

[93] Kimsey-House, H., Kimsey-House, K., Sandahl, P., and Whitworth, L. 2018. *Co-Active Coaching*. Nicholas Brealey.

[94] Northouse, P. G. 2013. *Leadership Theory and Practice*. Sage.

[95] Moseley, A. 2011. *Coaching ROI: Delivering Strategic Value Employing Executive Coaching in Defense Acquisition*. Xlibris Corporation, p. 99.

[96] Welch, J. 2005. *Winning*. HarperCollins.

[97] Goleman, D. 2011. What makes a leader? In *HBR's 10 must reads on leadership*. (pp. 1–22). Harvard Business Review Press.

[98] Hunt, J. M. and Weintraub, J. R. 2007. *From The Coaching Organization*. Sage.

[99] Moseley, A. 2011. *Coaching ROI: Delivering Strategic Value Employing Executive Coaching in Defense Acquisition*. Xlibris Corporation, p. 99.

[100] Goleman, D. 2011. What makes a leader? In *HBR's 10 must reads on leadership*. (pp. 1–22). Harvard Business Review Press.

[101] Passmore, J. 2012. *Psychometrics in Coaching: Using psychological and psychometric tools for development*. Kogan Page Limited.

[102] Herd, A. M., Alagaraja, M., and Cumberland, D. M. 2016. Assessing global leadership competencies: The critical role of assessment centre methodology. *Human Resource Development International*, 19(1), 27–43.

[103] Passmore, J. 2012. *Psychometrics in Coaching: Using psychological and psychometric tools for development*, Kogan Page Limited.

[104] Bazerman, M. H. and Tenbrunsel, A. E. 2011. *Blind Spots*. Princeton University Press.

[105] Rath, T. 2008. *Strengths based Leadership*. Gallup Press.

106 Collins, G. R. 2009. *Christian Coaching: Helping Others Turn Potential into Reality.* NavPress, p. 163.

107 Stoltzfus, T. 2005. *Leadership coaching: The disciplines, skills and heart of a Christian coach.* NavPress.

108 Bekker, C. J. 2009. Leading with the Head bowed down: Lessons in Leadership Humility from the Rule of St. Benedict of Nursia. *Inner Resources for Leaders.* Retrieved from

http://www.regent.edu/acad/global/publications/innerresources/vol1is s3/bekker_inspirational.pdf.

109 Stoltzfus, T. 2005. *Leadership coaching: The disciplines, skills and heart of a Christian coach.* NavPress.

110 Northouse, P. G. 2013. *Leadership Theory and Practice.* Sage, p. 319.

111 Johnson, C. E. and Hackman, M. Z. 2018. *Leadership a Communication Perspective.* Waveland Press.

112 Loehr, J. and Schwartz, T. 2003. *The Power of Full Engagement.* Free Press, p. 5.

113 Reuven, B. 2002. *BarOn Emotional Quotient Inventory.* Multi-Health Systems Inc.

114 Stoltzfus, T. 2005. *Leadership coaching: The disciplines, skills, and heart of a Christian coach.* NavPress.

115 Covey, S. R. 2004. *The 7 Habits of Highly Effective People.* Simon & Schuster.

116 Crane, T. G. 2017. *The heart of coaching: Using transformational coaching to create a high-performance culture.* FTA Press. p. 32.

117 DellaVecchio, D. and Winston, B. E., 2004. Roman 12 Instruments Working Paper, Regent University School of leadership studies.

118 DellaVecchio and Winston. 2004.

119 Winston, B. E. 2009. The Romans 12 Gifts: Useful for person-job fit, *Journal of Biblical perspectives in leadership*, 2, 114–134.

120 Winston. 2009.

121 Simmons, A. L. 2018. *Leadership Plan for Aspiring Leaders.* [Unpublished manuscript].

122 Winston, B. E. 2009. The Romans 12 Gifts: Useful for person-job fit, *Journal of Biblical perspectives in leadership*, 2, 114–134.

123 Simmons, A. L. 2018. *Leadership Plan for Aspiring Leaders.* [Unpublished manuscript].

124 DellaVecchio, D. and Winston, B. E. 2004. Roman 12 Instruments Working Paper, Regent University School of leadership studies.

125 Rath, T. 2008. *Strengths based Leadership.* Gallup Press.

126 Simmons, A. L. 2018. *Leadership Plan for Aspiring Leaders.* [Unpublished manuscript].

127 Bazerman, M. H. and Tenbrunsel, A. E. 2011. *Blind Spots.* Princeton University Press.

128 Denning, S. 2007. *The Secret Language of Leadership.* John Wiley & Sons.

129 Fedler, K. K. 2006. *Exploring Christian Ethics: Biblical Foundations for Morality.* Westminster John Knox Press.

130 Bazerman, M. H. and Tenbrunsel, A. E. 2011. *Blind Spots.* Princeton University Press.

131 Fedler, K. K. 2006. *Exploring Christian Ethics: Biblical Foundations for Morality*. Westminster John Knox Press.

132 Goleman, D. 2011. What makes a leader? In *HBR's 10 must reads on leadership*. (pp. 1–22). Harvard Business Review Press.

133 Baron, R.A and Byrne, D. 1997. *Social psychology (8th ed.)*. Allyn and Bacon.

134 Hultman, K. and Gellerman, B. 2002. *Balancing Individual and Organizational Values*. Jossey-Bass/Pfeifer.

135 Maslow, A. H. 1954. *Motivation and Personality*. Harper and Row.

136 Hultman, K. and Gellerman, B. 2002. *Balancing Individual and Organizational Values*. Jossey-Bass/Pfeifer.

137 Hultman and Gellerman, 2002.

138 Simmons, A. L. 2020. *Coaching in Organizations can right the onslaught of Upside-down Leadership*. [Unpublished manuscript].

139 Hultman, K. and Gellerman, B. 2002. *Balancing Individual and Organizational Values*. Jossey-Bass/Pfeifer.

140 Van Velsor, E., McCauley, C., and Ruderman, M. 2010. *Handbook of Leadership Development. (3rd ed.)*. Jossey-Bass.

141 Van Velsor, McCauley, and Ruderman. 2010.

142 Gaddis, B. H. and Foster, J. L. 2015. Meta-Analysis of dark side personality characteristics and critical work behaviors among leaders across the globe: Findings and implications for leadership development and executive coaching. *Applied Psychology, 64*(1), 25–54.

143 Hultman, K. and Gellerman, B. 2002. *Balancing Individual and Organizational Values*. Jossey-Bass/Pfeifer. p. 61.

144 Hultman and Gellerman, 2002.

145 Rokeach, M. 1973. *The Nature of Human Values*. The Free Press.

146 Rokeach. 1973.

147 Hultman, K. and Gellerman, B. 2002. *Balancing Individual and Organizational Values*. Jossey-Bass/Pfeifer.

148 Hultman and Gellerman, 2002.

149 Hultman and Gellerman, 2002.

150 Northouse, P. G. 2013. *Leadership Theory and Practice*. Sage.

151 Rothwell W. J. 2016. *Effective Succession Planning Fifth Edition*. AMACOM.

152 Schein, E. H. and Schein, P. 2017. *Organizational Culture and Leadership*. John Wiley & Sons.

153 Indeed Editorial Team. August 27, 2021. *5 Generations in the Workplace: Their Values and Differences*. Retrieved from: https://www.indeed.com/career-advice/career-development/generations-in-the-workplace.

154 Kouzes, J. and Posner, B. 2017. *The leadership challenge 6th ed*. John Wiley and Sons.

155 Kampf, R., Lorincová, S., Hitka, M., and Stopka, O. 2017. Generational differences in the perception of corporate culture in European transport enterprises. *Sustainability, 9*(9), 15–61.

156 Kampf, Lorincová, Hitka, and Stopka, 2017.

157 Hofstede, G., Hofstede, G., and Minkov, M. 2010. *Cultures and Organizations: Software of the Mind*. McGraw-Hill.

158 Hofstede, Hofstede, and Minkov. 2010.

[159] Schein, E. H. and Schein, P. 2017. *Organizational Culture and Leadership*. John Wiley & Sons.

[160] Bazerman, M. H. and Tenbrunsel, A. E., 2011. *Blind Spots*. Princeton University Press.

[161] Hultman, K. and Gellerman, B. 2002. *Balancing Individual and Organizational Values*. Jossey-Bass/Pfeifer.

[162] Lingenfelter, S. G. 1998. *Transforming Culture: A Challenge for Christian Mission*. Baker Academic.

[163] Bazerman, M. H. and Tenbrunsel, A. E. 2011. *Blind Spots*. Princeton University Press.

[164] Northouse, P. G. 2013. *Leadership Theory and Practice*. Sage.

[165] Northouse. 2013.

[166] Ciulla, J. B. 2014. *Ethics, the heart of leadership*. Praeger.

[167] Fedler, K. K. 2006. *Exploring Christian Ethics: Biblical Foundations for Morality*. Westminster John Knox Press.

[168] Bazerman, M. H. and Tenbrunsel, A. E., 2011. *Blind Spots*. Princeton University Press.

[169] Bazerman and Tenbrunsel. 2011. p. 73.

[170] Chatterjee, D. 2006. Wise Ways: Leadership as Relationship. *Journal of Human Values*, 12(2), 153–160.

[171] Bazerman, M. H. and Tenbrunsel, A. E., 2011. *Blind Spots*. Princeton University Press.

[172] Steib, M. 2018. *The Career Manifesto: discover your calling and create an extraordinary life*. Penguin Random House.

[173] Bond, W. 2019 *Swim! how a shark, a suckerfish, and a parasite teach you leadership, mentoring, &next level success*. Wiley, p. 59.

[174] Van Velsor, E., McCauley, C., and Ruderman, M. 2010. *Handbook of Leadership Development*. *(3rd ed.)*. Jossey-Bass, p. 17.

[175] Palmer, S. and Whybrow, A. 2019. *Handbook of Coaching Psychology*. Routledge. p. 27.

[176] Rankin, B. 2013. Emotional intelligence: Enhancing values-based practice and compassionate care in nursing. *Journal of Advanced Nursing, 69*(12), 2717–2725.

[177] Bazerman, M. H. and Tenbrunsel, A. E., 2011. *Blind Spots*. Princeton University Press, pp. 38–39.

[178] Bazerman and Tenbrunsel. 2011. p. 139.

[179] Chatterjee, D. 2006. Wise Ways: Leadership as Relationship. *Journal of Human Values*, 12(2), 153–160.

[180] Denning, S. 2007. *The Secret Language of Leadership*. Jossey-Bass, p. 57.

[181] Bazerman, M. H. and Tenbrunsel, A. E. 2011. *Blind Spots*. Princeton University Press.

[182] Van Velsor, E., McCauley, C., & Ruderman, M. 2010. *Handbook of Leadership Development*. *(3rd ed.)*, Jossey-Bass.

[183] Van Velsor, McCauley & Ruderman, 2010.

[184] Wasson, K. May 7, 2020. Social Intelligence for Project Mangers – Cat Herding 101. PMI on-Demand Webinars, Retrieved from

https://www.projectmanagement.com/videos/630836/Social-Intelligence-for-Project-Managers---Cat-Herding-101.

[185] Wells, J. E. and Aicher, T. J. 2013. Follow the leader: A relational demography, similarity attraction, and social identity theory of leadership approach of a team's performance. *Gender Issues, 30*(1–4), 1–14.

[186] Bazerman, M. H. and Tenbrunsel, A. E. 2011. *Blind Spots*. Princeton University Press.

[187] Mattis, J. and West, B. 2019. *Call Sign Chaos: Learning to Lead*. Random House.

[188] Mattis and West. 2019. p. 172.

[189] Northouse, P. G. 2013. *Leadership Theory and Practice*. Sage.

[190] Bazerman, M. H. and Tenbrunsel, A. E. 2011. *Blind Spots*. Princeton University Press.

[191] Fedler, K. K. 2006. *Exploring Christian Ethics: Biblical Foundations for Morality*. Westminster John Knox Press.

[192] Stanovich, K.E. and West, R.F. 2000. Individual Differences in Reasoning: Implications for the Rationality Debate, *Behavioral & Brain Sciences*, 23, 645–665.

[193] Kahneman, D. 2003. A Perspective on Judgment and Choice: Mapping Bounded Rationality, *American Psychologist*, 58, 697–720.

[194] Bazerman, M. H. and Tenbrunsel, A. E., 2011. *Blind Spots*. Princeton University Press, p. 172.

[195] Engstrom, T. W. 1976. *The Making of a Christian Leader*. Zondervan.

[196] Fedler, K. K. 2006. *Exploring Christian Ethics: Biblical Foundations for Morality*. Westminster John Knox Press.

[197] Fedler. 2006.

[198] Fedler. 2006.

[199] Fedler. 2006.

[200] Fedler. 2006.

[201] Cabrera, A. and Unruh, G. 2012. *Being Global: How to Think, Act, and Lead in a Transformed World*. Harvard Business Review.

[202] Nouwen, H. J. 1989. *In the Name of Jesus*. Crossroads Publishing.

[203] Fedler, K. K. 2006. *Exploring Christian Ethics: Biblical Foundations for Morality*. Westminster John Knox Press.

[204] Stoltzfus, T. 2005. *Leadership coaching: The disciplines, skills, and heart of a Christian coach*. NavPress.

[205] Stoltzfus. 2005.

[206] Stoltzfus. 2005.

[207] Kimsey-House, H., Kimsey-House, K., Sandahl, P., and Whitworth, L. 2018. *Co-Active Coaching*. Nicholas Brealey.

[208] Crane, T. G. 2017. *The heart of coaching: Using transformational coaching to create a high-performance culture*. FTA Press.

[209] Johnson, C. E. and Hackman, M. Z. 2018. *Leadership a Communication Perspective*. Waveland Press.

[210] Northouse, P. G. 2013. *Leadership Theory and Practice*. Sage.

[211] Robbins, V. K. 1996. *Exploring the Texture of Texts*. Bloomsbury Publishing.

[212] Rath, T. 2008. *Strengths based Leadership*. Gallup Press.

213 Stoltzfus, T. 2005. *Leadership coaching: The disciplines, skills and heart of a Christian coach.* NavPress.

214 Kouzes, J. and Posner, B. 2017. *The leadership challenge 6th ed.* John Wiley and Sons.

215 Johnson, C. E. and Hackman, M. Z. 2018. *Leadership a Communication Perspective.* Waveland Press.

216 Kimsey-House, H., Kimsey-House, K., Sandahl, P., and Whitworth, L. 2018. *Co-Active Coaching.* Nicholas Brealey.

217 Stoltzfus, T. 2005. *Leadership coaching: The disciplines, skills and heart of a Christian coach.* NavPress.

218 2005. "Curtis Fine Papers aligns strategy and leadership style with business priorities: Three pillars of development for top executives." *Human Resource Management Digest*, 13(6), 3–35.

219 Stoltzfus, T. 2005. *Leadership coaching: The disciplines, skills and heart of a Christian coach*, NavPress, Simmons, A. L. 2020. *Coaching Assessment and Strategic Development Plan.* [Unpublished manuscript].753M.

220 Palmer, S. and Whybrow, A. 2019. *Handbook of Coaching Psychology.* Routledge.

221 Palmer and Whybrow. 2019.

222 Stoltzfus, T. 2008. *Coaching Questions: A Coach's Guide to Powerful Asking Skills.* Pegasus Creative Arts.

223 Northouse, P. G. 2013. *Leadership Theory and Practice.* Sage, p. 186.

224 Crane, T. G. 2017. *The heart of coaching: Using transformational coaching to create a high-performance culture.* FTA Press, p. 31.

225 Collins, G. R. 2009. *Christian Coaching: Helping Others Turn Potential into Reality.* NavPress.

226 Stoltzfus, T. 2005. *Leadership coaching: The disciplines, skills, and heart of a Christian coach.* NavPress, pp. 4–21.

227 Hooker, T. 2013. Peer Coaching: A review of the literature. *Waikato Journal of Education*, 18(2), 129–139.

228 Kouzes, J. and Posner, B. 2017. *The leadership challenge 6th ed.* John Wiley and Sons.

229 Collins, G. R. 2009. *Christian Coaching: Helping Others Turn Potential into Reality.* NavPress.

230 Stoltzfus, T. 2005. *Leadership coaching: The disciplines, skills and heart of a Christian coach.* NavPress.

231 Stoltzfus. 2005.

232 Johnson, C. E. and Hackman, M. Z. 2018. *Leadership a Communication Perspective.* Waveland Press, p. 208.

233 Crane, T. G. 2017. *The heart of coaching: Using transformational coaching to create a high-performance culture.* FTA Press, p. 35.

234 Goleman, D. 2005. *Emotional Intelligence; why it can matter more than IQ.* Bantam Dell.

235 Stoltzfus, T. 2005. *Leadership coaching: The disciplines, skills and heart of a Christian coach.* NavPress.

236 Kouzes, J. and Posner, B. 2017. *The leadership challenge 6th ed.* John Wiley and Sons.

237 Simmons, A. L. 2020. *A Coaching Conversation Flatten Social Identity to Facilitate Global Leadership.* [Unpublished manuscript].

238 Van Velsor, E., McCauley, C., and Ruderman, M. 2010. *Handbook of Leadership Development.* 3rd ed.). Jossey-Bass.

REFERENCE

---

239 Collins, G. R. 2009. *Christian Coaching: Helping Others Turn Potential into Reality.* NavPress.

240 Stoltzfus, T. 2005. *Leadership coaching: The disciplines, skills and heart of a Christian coach.* NavPress.

241 Hunt, J. M. and Weintraub, J. R. 2007. *From The Coaching Organization.* Sage.

242 Hultman, K. and Gellerman, B. 2002. *Balancing Individual and Organizational Values.* Jossey- Bass/Pfeifer.

243 Passmore, J. 2012. *Psychometrics in Coaching: Using psychological and psychrometric tools for development.* Kogan Page Limited.

244 Northouse, P. G. 2013. *Leadership Theory and Practice.* Sage.

245 Cabrera, A. and Unruh, G. 2012. *Being Global: How to Think, Act, and Lead in a Transformed World.* Harvard Business Review.

246 Cabrera and Unruh. 2012.

247 Cabrera and Unruh. 2012.

248 Simmons, A. L. 2020. *Developing Military Leaders Across Cultures through Faith-based Democratic Leadership.* [Unpublished manuscript]. 733M.

249 Caligiuri, P. 2012. *Cultural Agility; Building a Pipeline of Successful Global Professionals.* Jossey-Bass.
Schein, E. H. 2010. *Organizational Culture and Leadership.* John Wiley & Sons.

250 Cabrera, A. and Unruh, G. 2012. *Being Global: How to Think, Act, and Lead in a Transformed World.* Harvard Business Review.

251 Cabrera and Unruh. 2012.

252 Caligiuri, P. 2012. *Cultural Agility; Building a Pipeline of Successful Global Professionals.* Jossey-Bass.
Simmons, A. L. 2019. *Cultural Intelligence yield Agnostic Global Leaders that are Culturally Agile.* [Unpublished manuscript].

253 Schein, E. H. and Schein, P. 2017. *Organizational Culture and Leadership.* John Wiley & Sons.

254 Caligiuri, P. 2012. *Cultural Agility; Building a Pipeline of Successful Global Professionals.* Jossey-Bass.

255 Hofstede, G., Hofstede, G., and Minkov, M. 2010. *Cultures and Organizations: Software of the Mind.* McGraw-Hill.

256 Lingenfelter, S. G. 2008. *Leading Cross-Culturally.* Baker Academic.

257 Collins, G. R. 2009. *Christian Coaching: Helping Others Turn Potential into Reality.* NavPress, p. 315.

258 Hofstede, G., Hofstede, G., and Minkov, M. 2010. *Cultures and Organizations: Software of the Mind.* McGraw-Hill.

259 Robbins, V. K. 1996. *Exploring the Texture of Texts.* Bloomsbury Publishing.

260 Darvishmotevali, M., Altinay, L., and De Vita, G. 2018. Emotional intelligence and creative performance: Looking through the lens of environmental uncertainty and cultural intelligence. *International Journal of Hospitality Management, 73,* 44–54.

261 Cameron, K. S. and Quinn, R. E. 2011. *Diagnosing and Changing Organizational Culture.* Wiley and Sons.

262 Hofstede, G. 2011. Dimensionalizing Cultures: The Hofstede Model in Context. *Online Readings in Psychology and Culture, 2*(1).

263 Cameron, K. S. and Quinn, R. E. 2011. *Diagnosing and Changing Organizational Culture.* Wiley and Sons.
Hofstede, G. 2011. Dimensionalizing Cultures: The Hofstede Model in Context. *Online Readings in Psychology and Culture, 2*(1).
264 Cameron and Quinn. 2011. Hofstede. 2011.
265 Cameron, K. S. and Quinn, R. E. 2011. *Diagnosing and Changing Organizational Culture.* Wiley and Sons, p. 84.
266 Chatterjee, D. 2006. Wise Ways: Leadership as Relationship. *Journal of Human Values,* 12(2), 153–160.
267 Schneider, W. E. 1994. Why Good Management Ideas Fail: the neglected power of organizational culture. *Strategy and Leadership,* 28(1), 24–29.
268 Divine, M. 2018. *The Way of the Seal.* Reader's Digest Publishing.
269 Divine. 2018.
270 Divine. 2018.
271 Cabrera, A. and Unruh, G. 2012. *Being Global: How to Think, Act, and Lead in a Transformed World.* Harvard Business Review.
272 Caligiuri, P. 2012. *Cultural Agility; Building a Pipeline of Successful Global Professionals.* Jossey-Bass.
273 Caligiuri, P. 2012. *Cultural Agility; Building a Pipeline of Successful Global Professionals.* Jossey-Bass.
274 Cabrera, A. and Unruh, G. 2012. *Being Global: How to Think, Act, and Lead in a Transformed World.* Harvard Business Review.
275 Caligiuri, P. 2012. *Cultural Agility; Building a Pipeline of Successful Global Professionals.* Jossey-Bass.
276 Suderman, J. September 10, 2019. *DSL 727 Period 2 Live Orientation.* Retrieved from https://us.bbcollab.com/collab/ui/session/playback.
277 Bazerman, M. H. and Tenbrunsel, A. E. 2011. *Blind Spots.* Princeton University Press.
278 Caligiuri, P. 2012. *Cultural Agility; Building a Pipeline of Successful Global Professionals.* Jossey-Bass.
279 Schein, E. H. and Schein, P. 2017. *Organizational Culture and Leadership.* John Wiley & Sons.
280 Caligiuri, P. 2012. *Cultural Agility; Building a Pipeline of Successful Global Professionals.* Jossey-Bass.
281 Schein, E. H. and Schein, P. 2017. *Organizational Culture and Leadership.* John Wiley & Sons.
282 Mattis, J. and West, B. 2019. *Call Sign Chaos: Learning to Lead.* Random House, p. 197.
283 Dastmalchian, A., Lee, S., and Ng, I. 2001. The Interplay between Organizational and National Cultures. *The International Journal of Human Resource Management,* 11(2), 388–412. Simmons, A. L. 2019. *Let your Values & Culture make your Organization Problem-Free.* [Unpublished manuscript].
284 Perkins, A. W. 2009. Global Leadership Study: A Theoretical Framework. *Journal of Leadership Education,* 8(2), 72–83.

[285]Dickson, M. W., Den Hartog, D. N., and Mitchelson, J. K. 2003. Research on leadership in a cross-cultural context: Making progress and raising new questions. *The Leadership Quarterly, 14*(6), 729–768.

[286] Cabrera, A. and Unruh, G. 2012. *Being Global: How to Think, Act, and Lead in a Transformed World.* Harvard Business Review.

[287] Lingenfelter, S. G. 2008. *Leading Cross-Culturally.* Baker Academic.

[288] Johnson, C. E. and Hackman, M. Z. 2018. *Leadership a Communication Perspective.* Waveland Press.

[289] Lingenfelter, S. G. 2008. *Leading Cross-Culturally.* Baker Academic.

[290] Cabrera, A. and Unruh, G. 2012. *Being Global: How to Think, Act, and Lead in a Transformed World.* Harvard Business Review.

[291] Cabrera and Unruh. 2012.

[292] Perkins, A. W. 2009. Global Leadership Study: A Theoretical Framework. *Journal of Leadership Education,* 8(2), 72–83.

[293] Caligiuri, P. 2012. *Cultural Agility; Building a Pipeline of Successful Global Professionals.* Jossey-Bass.

[294] Caligiuri. 2012.

[295] Caligiuri. 2012.

[296] Caligiuri. 2012.

[297] Caligiuri. 2012.

[298] Caligiuri. 2012.

[299] Caligiuri. 2012.

[300] Stambulova, N. B. 2009. Putting culture into context: Cultural and cross-cultural perspectives in career development and transition research and practice. *International Journal of Sports and Exercise Psychology,* 7(3), 292–308.

[301] Cabrera, A. and Unruh, G. 2012. *Being Global: How to Think, Act, and Lead in a Transformed World.* Harvard Business Review.

[302] Caligiuri, P. 2012. *Cultural Agility; Building a Pipeline of Successful Global Professionals.* Jossey-Bass.

[303] Hofstede, G., Hofstede, G., and Minkov, M. 2010. *Cultures and Organizations: Software of the Mind.* McGraw-Hill.

[304] Hofstede, Hofstede, and Minkov. 2010.

[305] Cabrera, A. and Unruh, G. 2012. *Being Global: How to Think, Act, and Lead in a Transformed World.* Harvard Business Review.

[306] Hofstede, G., Hofstede, G., and Minkov, M. 2010. *Cultures and Organizations: Software of the Mind.* McGraw-Hill.

[307] Caligiuri, P. 2012. *Cultural Agility; Building a Pipeline of Successful Global Professionals.* Jossey-Bass.

[308] Cabrera, A. and Unruh, G. 2012. *Being Global: How to Think, Act, and Lead in a Transformed World.* Harvard Business Review.

[309] Cabrera and Unruh. 2012.

[310] Caligiuri, P. 2012. *Cultural Agility; Building a Pipeline of Successful Global Professionals.* Jossey-Bass, p. 54.

[311] Cabrera, A. and Unruh, G. 2012. *Being Global: How to Think, Act, and Lead in a Transformed World.* Harvard Business Review.

[312]Cabrera and Unruh. 2012.

313 Hunt, J. M. and Weintraub, J. R. 2007. *The Coaching Organization: A strategy for developing leaders.* Sage.

314 Anderson, D. and Anderson, M. 2005. *Coaching That Counts.* Elsevier Butterworth-Heinemann.

315 Hunt, J. M. and Weintraub, J. R. 2007. *The Coaching Organization: A strategy for developing leaders.* Sage.

316 Stokes, C. October 14, 2019. *7 Work Trends You Should be Paying Attention to* [Blog Post]. Retrieved from: https://blog.shrm.org/blog/7-work-trends-you-should-be-paying-attention-to.

317 Ciulla, J. B. 2014. *Ethics, the heart of leadership.* Praeger.

318 Moseley, A. 2011. *Coaching ROI: Delivering Strategic Value Employing Executive Coaching in Defense Acquisition.* Xlibris Corporation, p. 24.

319 Anderson, D. and Anderson, M. 2005. *Coaching That Counts.* Elsevier Butterworth-Heinemann.

320 Simmons, A. L. 2020. Coach to be Coached: optimizing technology and human skills. [Unpublished manuscript].

321 Collins, G. R. 2009. *Christian Coaching: Helping Others Turn Potential into Reality.* NavPress.

322 Phillips, T. 2011. Creating a coaching culture across a global sales force. *Strategic HR Review,* 10(4), 5–10.

323 Crane, T. G. 2017. *The heart of coaching: Using transformational coaching to create a high-performance culture.* FTA Press.

324 Amanchukwu, R. N., Stanley, G. J., and Ololube, N. P. 2015. A Review of Leadership Theories, Principles and Styles and Their Relevance to Educational Management. *Management,* 5(1), 6–14. Simmons, A. L. 2020. *Literature Review of Executive Leadership Coaching in the Global Defense Sector.* [Unpublished manuscript].

325 Collins, G. R. 2009. *Christian Coaching: Helping Others Turn Potential into Reality.* NavPress.

326 John, D. and Paisner, D. 2020. *POWERSHIFT: Transform any Situation, Close Any Deal, and Achieve Any Outcome.* Currency.

327 Palmer, S. and Whybrow, A. 2019. *Handbook of Coaching Psychology.* Routledge, p. 27.

328 Bennis, W. 1999. The End of Leadership: Exemplary Leadership is impossible without full inclusion, initiatives, and cooperation of Followers, *Organizational Dynamics,* 28, 71–79.

329 Schneider, W. E. 1994. Why Good Management Ideas Fail: the neglected power of organizational culture. *Strategy and Leadership,* 28(1), 24–29.

330 Ali, M., Zhang, L., Shah, S. J., Khan, S., and Shah, A. M. 2020. Impact of humble leadership on project success: The mediating role of psychological empowerment and innovative work behavior. *Leadership & Organization Development Journal,* 41(3), 349–367.

331 Ali, Zhang, Shah, Khan, Shah. 2020.

332 Maxwell, J. C. 2020. *The Leader's Greatest Return: attracting, developing, and multiplying leaders.* HarperCollins.

333 Northouse, P. G. 2013. *Leadership Theory and Practice.* Sage.

REFERENCE

[334] Overstreet, R. L. 2015. EGO vs. EQ: How Top Leaders Beat 8 EGO Traps with Emotional Intelligence, *Journal of Applied Christian Leadership*, 9, 110–112.

[335] Williams, W. A., Brandon, R. S., Hayek, M., Haden, S. P., and Atinc, G. 2017. Servant leadership and followership creativity: The influence of workplace spirituality and political skill. *Leadership & Organization Development Journal*.

[336] Uhl-Bien, M. et al. 2014. Followership Theory: A Review and Research Agenda, *The Leadership Quarterly*, 25, 83–104

[337] Bennis, W. 1999. The End of Leadership: Exemplary Leadership is impossible without full inclusion, initiatives, and cooperation of Followers, *Organizational Dynamics*, 28, 71–79.

[338] Warren, R. 2002. *The Purpose Drive Life: What on Earth Am I Here For?* Zondervan.

[339] [Simmons, A. L. 2018. *Leadership Plan for Aspiring Leaders.* Unpublished manuscript].

[340] Kouzes, J. and Posner, B. 2017. *The leadership challenge 6th ed.* John Wiley and Sons.

[341] Kouzes and Posner. 2017.

[342] Brady, J. 2000. *The Coldest War: A Memoir of Korea.* St. Martin's Press.

[343] Kouzes, J. and Posner, B. 2017. *The leadership challenge 6th ed.* John Wiley and Sons.

[344] Hofstede, G., Hofstede, G., and Minkov, M. 2010. *Cultures and Organizations: Software of the Mind.* New York: NY: McGraw-Hill.

[345] Kouzes, J. and Posner, B. 2017. *The leadership challenge 6th ed.* John Wiley and Sons, p. 15.

[346] Hughes, R. L., Beatty, K. C., and Dinwoodie, D. L. 2014. p. 231.

[347] Kouzes, J. and Posner, B. 2017. *The leadership challenge 6th ed.* John Wiley and Son, p. 250.

[348] Denning, S. 2007. *The Secret Language of Leadership.* John Wiley & Sons, p. 57.

[349] Kouzes, J. and Posner, B. 2017. *The leadership challenge 6th ed.* John Wiley and Son, p. 17.

[350] Kouzes and Posner. 2017.

[351] Northouse, P. G. 2013. *Leadership Theory and Practice.* Sage.

[352] Chaleff. 1996.

[353] Kouzes, J. and Posner, B. 2017. *The leadership challenge 6th ed.* John Wiley and Son.

[354] Simmons, A. L. 2020. *Developing Military Leaders Across Cultures through Faith-based Democratic Leadership.* [Unpublished manuscript].

[355] Moseley, A. 2011. *Coaching ROI: Delivering Strategic Value Employing Executive Coaching in Defense Acquisition.* Xlibris Corporation.

[356] Blackbyrn, A. January 15, 2020. The Coach Accelerator [Webinar]. *In LLC Webinar Series.* Retrieved from https://events.genndi.com/lve/818182175026321098/378fdd5704/jot/173149392.

[357] María Martínez-León, I., and Martínez-García, J. A. 2011. The influencing of organizational structure on organizational learning. *International Journal of Manpower*, 32(5/6), 537–566.

[358] Cameron, K. S. and Quinn, R. E. 2011. *Diagnosing and Changing Organizational Culture.* Wiley and Sons.

[359] Cameron and Quinn. 2011.

360 María Martínez-León, I. and Martínez-García, J. A. 2011. The influencing of organizational structure on organizational learning. *International Journal of Manpower*, 32(5/6), 537–566.

361 Kouzes, J. and Posner, B. 2017. *The leadership challenge 6th ed.* John Wiley and Son.

362 Kouzes and Posner. 2017.

363 Schneider, W. E. 1994. Why Good Management Ideas Fail: the neglected power of organizational culture. *Strategy and Leadership*, 28(1), 24–29.

364 Kouzes, J. and Posner, B. 2017. *The leadership challenge 6th ed.* John Wiley and Son.

365 María Martínez-León, I. and Martínez-García, J. A. 2011. The influencing of organizational structure on organizational learning. *International Journal of Manpower*, 32(5/6), 537–566.

366 Van Velsor, E., McCauley, C., and Ruderman, M. 2010. *Handbook of Leadership Development.* (3rd ed.). Jossey-Bass.

367 Zhou, F. and Wu, Y. J. 2018. How humble leadership fosters employee innovation behavior: A two-way perspective on the leader-employee interaction. *Leadership & Organization Development Journal*, 39(3), 375–387.

368 Zhou and Wu. 2018.

369 Burton, R. M., Obel, B., and Hakonsson, D. D. 2015. *Organizational Design: a step-by-step approach,* Cambridge University Press.

370 Uhl-Bien, M. et al. 2014. Followership Theory: A Review and Research Agenda, *The Leadership Quarterly*, 25, 83–104.

371 Aska, J. Dec 22, 2018. *Schools Now Vs. 20 Years Ago: 20 Things That Have Changed. From social stigma and cliques to the way a class is taught, many things have evolved and changed.* Retrieved from Schools Now Vs. 20 Years Ago: 20 Things That Have Changed (moms.com).

372 Lazzerini, L. November 16, 2021. The Concept of Shared Leadership. *PMI On-Demand Webinars,* Retrieved from http://www.projectmanagement.com/Webinars/webinarMainOnDemand.cfm.

373 Northouse, P. G. 2013. *Leadership Theory and Practice.* Sage.

374 Anderson, D. and Anderson, M. 2005. *Coaching That Counts.* Elsevier Butterworth-Heinemann.

375 Simmons, A. L. 2020. *Coach to be Coached: optimizing technology and human skills.* [Unpublished manuscript].

376 Maxwell, J. C. 2020. *The Leader's Greatest Return: attracting, developing, and multiplying leaders.* HarperCollins.

377 John, D. and Paisner, D. 2020. *POWERSHIFT: Transform any Situation, Close Any Deal, and Achieve Any Outcome.* Currency.

378 Cabrera, A. and Unruh, G. 2012. *Being Global: How to Think, Act, and Lead in a Transformed World.* Harvard Business Review.

379 Johnson, C. E. and Hackman, M. Z. 2018. *Leadership a Communication Perspective.* Waveland Press.

380 Amanchukwu, R. N., Stanley, G. J., and Ololube, N. P. 2015. A Review of Leadership Theories, Principles and Styles and Their Relevance to Educational Management. *Management*, 5(1), 6–14.

381 Johnson, C. E. and Hackman, M. Z. 2018. *Leadership a Communication Perspective.* Waveland Press.

[382] Johnson and Hackman. 2018. *Leadership a Communication Perspective*. Waveland Press.

[383] Rath, T. 2008. *Strengths based Leadership*. Gallup Press.

[384] Rath. 2008. p. 215.

[385] Kouzes, J. and Posner, B. 2017. The leadership challenge 6thed, John Wiley and Sons.

[386] Obama, B. 2020. *A Promised Land*. Crown.

[387] Bassett, S. 2012. Accountability in the NHS. *Nursing Management (Harrow, London, England: 1994)*, 19(8), 24.

[388] Covey, S. M. R and Merrill, R. R. 2006. *The Speed of Trust*. Simon & Schuster. p. XXV.

[389] Covey and Merrill. 2006.

[390] Bassett, S. 2012. Accountability in the NHS. *Nursing Management (Harrow, London, England: 1994)*, 19(8), 24.

[391] Bennis, W. 1999. The End of Leadership: Exemplary Leadership is impossible without full inclusion, initiatives, and cooperation of followers. *Organizational Dynamics*, 71–79.

[392] Kimsey-House, H., Kimsey-House, K., Sandahl, P., and Whitworth, L., 2018 *Co-Active Coaching*. Nicholas Brealey.

[393] Kouzes, J. and Posner, B. 2017. The leadership challenge 6thed, John Wiley and Sons.

[394] Carbery, R. and Cross, C. 2015. *Human Resource Development: A concise Introduction*. Palgrave.

[395] Simmons, A. L. 2020. *Coaching in Organizations can right the onslaught of Upside-down Leadership*. [Unpublished manuscript].

[396] Carbery, R. and Cross, C. 2015. *Human Resource Development: A concise Introduction*. Palgrave

[397] Carbery and Cross. 2015. pp. 120–121.

[398] Carbery and Cross. 2015.

[399] Friedman, T. 2016. Thank You for Being Late. Farrar, Straus and Giroux.

[400] Carbery and Cross. 2015.

[401] Carbery and Cross. 2015.

[402] Lingenfelter, S. G. 2008. *Leading Cross-Culturally*. Baker Academic, p. 165.

[403] Rothwell W. J. 2016. *Effective Succession Planning Fifth Edition*. AMACOM, p. 15.

[404] Dacquino, D. March 19, 2020. *Message from the CEO on COVID-2019*. Retrieved from
https://serco.kzoplatform.com/player/medium/1644338780674463124.

[405] Van Velsor, E., McCauley, C., and Ruderman, M. 2010. *Handbook of Leadership Development*. (3rd ed.). Jossey-Bass.

[406] Carbery, R. and Cross, C. 2015. *Human Resource Development: A concise Introduction*. Palgrave.

[407] Northouse, P. G. 2013. *Leadership Theory and Practice*. Sage.

[408] Cheung, S. Y., Gong, Y., and Huang, J. C. Emotional intelligence, job insecurity, and psychological strain among real estate agents: a test of mediation and moderation models. *International Journal of Human Resource Management*, [s. l.], v. 27, n. 22, p. 2673–2694, 2016.

409 McCauley, C., Kanaga, K., and Lafferty, K. 2010. Leader Development Systems. *In The Center for Creative Leadership Handbook of Leadership Development.* (pp. 29–62). Jossey-Bass.

410 Simmons, A. L. 2019. *Future of Human Resources - trends, reflections, and strategies.* [Unpublished manuscript].

411 Northouse, P. G. 2013. *Leadership Theory and Practice.* Sage.

412 Amanchukwu, R. N., Stanley, G. J., and Ololube, N. P., 2015. A Review of Leadership Theories, Principles and Styles and Their Relevance to Educational Management. *Management,* 5(1), 6–14.

413 Simmons, A. L. 2020. *Core-Flex Model: integrative approach to organizational leadership.* [Unpublished manuscript].

414 Carbery, R. and Cross, C. 2015. *Human Resource Development: A concise Introduction.* Palgrave.

415 Simmons, A. L. 2020. *Core-Flex Model: integrative approach to organizational leadership.* [Unpublished manuscript].

416 Simmons. 2020.

417 Carbery, R. and Cross, C. 2015. *Human Resource Development: A concise Introduction.* Palgrave.

418 Bennis, W. 1999. The End of Leadership: Exemplary Leadership is impossible without full inclusion, initiatives, and cooperation of followers. *Organizational Dynamics,* 71–79.

419 Simmons, A. L. 2018. *Preparing Sailor for Successful Engagements in the Global Maritime Domain.* [Unpublished manuscript].

420 Northouse, P. G. 2013. *Leadership Theory and Practice.* Sage.

421 Chatterjee, D. 2006. Wise Ways: Leadership as Relationship. *Journal of Human Values,* 12(2), 153–160.

422 Engstrom, T. W. 1976. *The Making of a Christian Leader.* Zondervan. Simmons, A. L. 2019. *Future of Human Resources—trends, reflections, and strategies.* [Unpublished manuscript].

423 Johnson, C. E. and Hackman, M. Z. 2018. *Leadership a Communication Perspective.* Waveland Press, p. 408.

424 Laiho, M. and Brandt, T. 2012. Views of HR specialists on formal mentoring: current situation and prospects for the future. *Career Development International.*

425 Carbery, R. and Cross, C. 2015. *Human Resource Development: A concise Introduction.* Palgrave.

426 Caligiuri, P. 2012. *Cultural Agility; Building a Pipeline of Successful Global Professionals.* Jossey-Bass.

427 Hunt, J. M. and Weintraub, J. R. 2007. *From The Coaching Organization.* Sage.

428 Moseley, A. 2011. *Coaching ROI: Delivering Strategic Value Employing Executive Coaching in Defense Acquisition.* Xlibris Corporation.

429 Simmons, A. L. 2019. *A Leader's Architecture for Creating a Shared Culture for Two Mergers.* [Unpublished manuscript].

430 Stokes, C. October 14, 2019. *7 Work Trends You Should be Paying Attention to* [Blog Post]. Retrieved from: https://blog.shrm.org/blog/7-work-trends-you-should-be-paying-attention-to.

[431] Crane, T. G. 2017. *The heart of coaching: Using transformational coaching to create a high-performance culture.* FTA Press.

[432] Goleman, D. 2011. What makes a leader? In *HBR's 10 must reads on leadership* (pp. 1–22). Harvard Business Review Press.

[433] Stokes, C. 2019, October 14. *7 Work Trends You Should be Paying Attention to* [Blog Post]. Retrieved from: https://blog.shrm.org/blog/7-work-trends-you-should-be-paying-attention-to.

[434] Goleman, D. 2011. What makes a leader? In *HBR's 10 must reads on leadership* (pp. 1–22). Harvard Business Review Press.

[435] Robison, J. Jan. 17, 2020. *Give Up Bossing, Take Up Coaching: You'll Like the Results.* Retrieved from: www.gallup.com/workplace/282647/give-bossing-coaching-results.aspx.

[436] Carter, J. 2015. *A Full Life: reflection at ninety*, Simon Schuster, p. 76.

[437] Simmons, A. L. 2020. *Coaching in Organizations can right the onslaught of Upside-down Leadership.* [Unpublished manuscript].

9 798348 118365